How to Win at BACKGAMMON

Books by Walter Gibson

Secret of Magic*
Magic with Science*
Stories from the Twilight Zone*
The Twilight Zone Revisited*
Hypnotism*
Dreams*
Witchcraft*
Weird Adventures of the Shadow*

The Fine Art of Murder
The Fine Art of Robbery
The Fine Art of Spying
The Fine Art of Swindling
Complete Book of Psychic Science
Complete Book of Divination and Prophecy
Hoyle's Encyclopedia of Card Games
Family Games America Plays
The Mystic and Occult Arts
Houdini's Escapes
Houdini's Magic

*Published by Grosset & Dunlap

How to Win at BACKGAMMON

by Walter Gibson

Originally published as *Fell's Guide to Winning Backgammon*

GROSSET & DUNLAP
A FILMWAYS COMPANY
Publishers • New York

Published by arrangement with Frederick Fell, Inc.
Originally published as *Fell's Guide to Winning Backgammon*
Published simultaneously in Canada
Library of Congress catalog card number: 77-93611
ISBN 0-448-14682-7
Printed in the United States of America
First Grosset & Dunlap Printing 1978

Contents

How to Win at BACKGAMMON

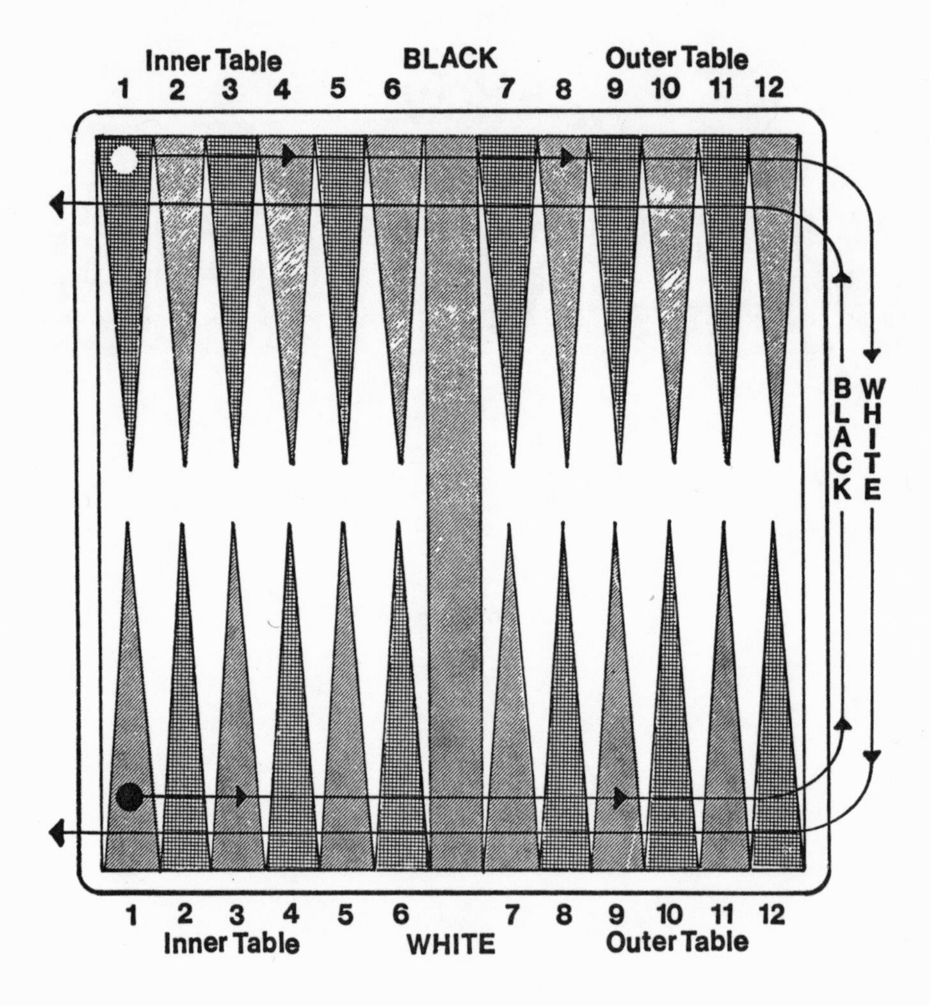
Inner Table
BLACK
Outer Table
1 2 3 4 5 6 7 8 9 10 11 12
BLACK
WHITE
1 2 3 4 5 6 7 8 9 10 11 12
Inner Table
WHITE
Outer Table

I

General Rules of Backgammon

FOR HUNDREDS OF YEARS, COUNTLESS THOUSANDS OF people have gazed upward into the night sky wondering what the other side of the moon looks like. At last, their curiosity has been satisfied. After exhaustive research and the expenditure of a few billion dollars, intrepid astronauts were enabled to circumnavigate the moon and bring back firsthand reports regarding its hitherto unseen hemisphere. That indeed is progress.

During those same centuries, countless thousands of chess and checker players have repeatedly seen the other side of the checkerboard without wondering what it was all about, and in many cases not even caring. It never occurred to most of them that they were acquiring, practically for free, most of the necessary implements for one of the keenest games of all time, backgammon, which not only deserves to be ranked with checkers or chess, but has unusual points of its own.

We say "almost for free," because a few additional items are needed; half a dozen extra checkers which may be borrowed from another set, and a pair of dice. With those at hand, you can start backgammoning at once, but if you prefer more elaborate accoutrements, you will find them readily available. These range from fancier boards to special tables; they include full quotas of backgammon pieces, or "stones" as they are traditionally called; they come with two pairs of dice and dice cups to go with them, one for each player; and also a more modern device, called a "doubling cube," regarded as essential when the game is played for high stakes.

All this means that backgammon is not only here to stay, but is apt to go places as well. It experienced one surge to popularity a generation ago and maintained its status in select circles during the years that followed. Now, with the promised leisure of the future calling for a revival of pastimes from the past, backgammon has again surged to the fore, and there is strong likelihood that if forthcoming space missions establish a lunar base on the other side of the moon, the astronauts stationed there will while away their time rolling dice and moving pieces on the other side of the checkerboard. That, too, will be progress.

How Backgammon Is Played

Backgammon is a game for two players, seated opposite. For convenience, one player is usually termed "Black" and the other "White," according to the color of the stones belonging to each. (These pieces may be the same as "checkers," which, as already stated, can be used in backgammon play, but the term "stones" belongs distinctively to backgammon, so will be used throughout.)

The board itself is divided into four quarters, called "tables," each with six long, pointed triangles, aptly termed "points." Each player has an "inner table" and an "outer table." In the diagram shown, Black, at the far end of the board, has his inner table on his right and his outer table on his left; while White, at the near end, has his inner table on his left and his outer table on his right. The inner and outer tables are separated by a dividing line known as the "bar," which runs from one end of the board to the other. The bar is simply a divider and in no way restricts the movement of the stones, which are moved from point to point, one at a time, in accordance with the totals that appear on the dice after a player rolls them.

The points themselves do not bear numbers on the standard backgammon board, but it is customary to refer to them as a player's 1-point (or ace-point), 2-point, 3-point, 4-point, 5-point, 6-point 7-point, (more commonly called his "bar-point"), and so on, up to his 12-point. These are so numbered in the diagrams that appear in the following pages and for quick reference. The points on Black's end of the board are listed as 1–B, 2–B, 3–B, and so on; while those at White's end are 1–W, 2–W, 3–W, and so on.

Thus Black's inner table consists of points 1–B to 6–B and Black's outer table includes points 7–B to 12–B, ranging from right to left, from Black's position. White's inner table consists of points 1–W to 6–W; and White's outer table includes points 7–W to 12–W, ranging from left to right, from White's position.

Each player has fifteen stones, and at the outset these are placed as follows: Two on the opposing 1-point; five on the opposing 12-point; three on the player's own 8-point; five on his own 6-point. These are shown in the accompanying diagram, from which it will be seen that Black has two stones on 1–W, five on 12–W, three on 8–B and five on 6–B; whereas White has two stones on 1–B, five on 12–B, three on 8–W and five on 6–W.

The direction of each player's moves is from the opponent's inner table to the opponent's outer table, then to the player's own outer table and from there to the player's own inner table. This is also indicated on the diagram, which clearly shows that Black's potential moves run in the order 1–W, 2–W, 3–W, 4–W, 5–W, 6–W, 7–W, 8–W, 9–W, 10–W, 12–W, 12–B, 11–B, 10–B, 9–B, 8–B, 7–B, 6–B, 5–B, 4–B, 3–B, 2–B, 1–B. In contrast, White's potential moves run: 1–B, 2–B, 2–B, 3–B, 4–B, 5–B, 6–B, 7–B, 8–B, 9–B, 10–B, 10–B, 11–B, 12–B, 12–W, 11–W, 10–W, 9–W, 8–W, 7–W, 6–W, 5–W, 4–W, 3–W, 2–W, 1–W.

The Objects of the Game

The main objects of the game are twofold: First, a player's aim is to move his men point by point until all fifteen are congregated in his own inner table, which is also known as his "home table." There is no limit to the number of men that a player can gather on a single point. The diagram shows how he starts with as many as five on a single point, and it would be theoretically possible for him to pile up all fifteen on his six-point, though this has probably never happened, as there would be no real purpose for it and it is highly unlikely that the dice would come up with all the rolls that would be required.

However, having accomplished his first aim of bringing all his stones to his inner table, the player's next and final objective is to "bear them off" by rolling the exact numbers required to move specific stones completely from the board. Thus a roll of 6 would permit Black to bear off a stone from his 6-point, 6–B, because a count of 5 would move the stone to 1–B and he would still have one more count to go. Similarly, a roll of 5 would enable a player to bear off a man from his 5-point; a roll of 4 from his 4-point, and so on.

There are a few special rules that apply to bearing off, which will be discussed in due course, but one to be kept firmly in mind all through the game is that a player *cannot* begin to bear off until *all* his men are occupying points on his inner table. That is a highly important feature of backgammon, so important in fact that some players take the mistaken attitude that "bearing off" is the *only* objective in the game. But since we have just stressed the fact that a player must first bring his men "home" in order to bear them off, the earlier objective becomes important in its own right; and careless tactics at that stage of the game may cause disaster later.

All this becomes very clear when close attention is given to the rules governing the moves of the stones according to the rolls of the dice, or "throws."

Throwing and Moving

Each player, in turn, throws the dice and moves his stones according to the numbers that turn up. In moving, a stone may touch any point in transit, but it cannot stop on a point occupied by two or more opposing stones. Furthermore, the numbers that turn up must be considered *singly,* so that the moves are made according to the spots showing on each individual die. This has an immediate effect on the play, as the following example will reveal:

Suppose that White has the opening roll and throws 5–1. For some reason, White wants to move a stone from 1–B to 6–B, by using the 5 throw; and also would like to move another from 12–B to 12–W, for the 1 throw. A nice idea, but White can't do it, as he is not allowed to put a stone on a point already controlled by two or more Blacks.

In contrast, White could use his 5–1 throw to move a stone from 12–B to 8–W, where it joins the three Whites already there. He still can't use the 1 to move from 12–B to 12–W, but he can apply it somewhere else. He could move a stone from 1–B to 2–B; or from 6–W to 5–W; or he could take the *same stone* that he moved from 12–B to 8–W and move it from 8–W to 7–W.

Another case: Suppose that Black has the opening roll and comes up with 5–4. For some reason he wants to move a stone from 1–W to 10–W, which seems quite simple. He could use the 5 to go from 1–W to 6–W; then the 4 to continue from 6–W to 10–W. However, he can't do it that way, because 6–W is already occupied by five of White's stones, and two would be enough to prevent Black from stopping there before continuing his play. But that is no real problem in this case. All that Black has to do is reverse the order of the dice. Instead of calling his throw 5–4, he treats it as 4–5. He uses his 4 to move from 1–W to 5–W and from there, he uses his 5 to move to 10–W.

Always, a player must use his full roll whenever he can, but as the game progresses, there may be times when he finds himself actually blocked by opposing men. If he can't use both numbers on the dice, he must use the larger if he can. If he can't use the larger, he must use the smaller, if he can. If he can't use either, he loses his roll and his opponent takes his turn.

Throwing Doubles

Whenever a player throws a double number such as 1–1, 2–2, etc, he gains double the number of moves. Thus with a roll of 1–1, instead of making two moves of one point each, he makes four such moves. With 2–2, he would make four moves of two each, and so on upward to 6–6, which represents the highest possible roll with four moves of six points each, or a total of 24.

Since these moves are made singly, they can be applied to one, two, three, or even four stones, as the player prefers. For instance, with double 4, a player could make any of the following moves:

One stone, a total of 16 points (4+4+4+4).

Two stones, a total of 8 points each (4+4 and 4+4).

One stone, four points; another a total of 12 (4+4+4).

One stone, a total of 8 points (4+4) and two others of four points each.

Four stones, a mere 4 points each.

Like other moves, these must all be treated singly, the actual difference being that with an ordinary roll (like 5–1) there are only two separate moves; whereas with "doubles" (like 3–3) there are four such moves. The same limitation applies in all cases: A player cannot terminate any of those single moves on a point occupied by two or more opposing stones. So as the game progresses, a player may sometimes find himself somewhat puzzled as to the best way to move his doubles.

One great advantage with doubles is that two stones can be moved together, thus establishing themselves on a new point, since each has moved exactly the same number. This brings up some interesting angles of play which come under the following head:

Blots, Builders, and Blocks

When a player is forced to move a stone to an unoccupied point, it is known as a "blot" and is vulnerable to enemy attack. To clarify this, assume that Black makes an opening roll of 5–1 and moves one stone from 12–W to 8–B; and another from 6–B to 5–B. The stone on 8–B is safe enough, as it has joined the Blacks already there, but the one on 5–B becomes a blot.

This means that if White makes a roll that puts one of his stones on that same point, it is termed a "hit" and the Black blot is banished from the board, being "sent to the bar," where it is out of play. On Black's next roll, he must reenter it, or lose his roll entirely. To reenter, Black rolls the dice and uses one of the numbers to reenter on the corresponding point of White's inner table. With a roll of 5–4, Black could reenter on either 4–W or 5–W and use the other number to move either that stone or another. However:

A stone cannot be reentered on a point already occupied by two or more of the opponent's stones. This conforms to the rule that a move cannot end on a point held by the opponent. But here, there is no alternative. If a player is unable to reenter, he cannot make a move. In the case just shown, with the game just underway, the only roll that would prevent Black from reentering would be a Double 6 (6–6), since White still has his five original stones on his 6-point (6–W). But as the game progresses and more stones clutter up the inner tables, the problem of reentering becomes more difficult and may ruin the hopes of an unwary player.

That raises the question in the average beginner's mind: Why take chances by forming blots whenever they can be avoided?

The answer is that a keen player frequently regards a blot as a calculated risk, which can pay handsome dividends if he gets away with it. To his way of thinking, the term "blot" is a misnomer. If he purposely moves a stone to an isolated and therefore vulnerable position, he prefers to think of it as a "builder" which forms the first step toward a "block" that will help cramp his opponent's play.

Again, consider the case where Black rolls a 5–1 and moves a stone from 12–W to 8–B, putting four on his 8-point; and moves another stone from 6–B to 5–B, where it becomes a blot—or preferably a builder!—on Black's 5-point. This is early in the game, so White still has two stones on Black's ace-point, 1–B, and therefore, if he rolls a 4, he can "hit" the Black "blot" and send it to the bar, killing its prospects as a "builder."

But unless White rolls a double 2 or a double 4, he will be forced to split his "runners" as his stones on 1–B are termed. If he should roll 4–3 and use the 4 to hit the Black blot, he would have to leave his other stone on 1–B and make another move elsewhere; or he would be forced to move it to 4–B, so White would then have *two* blots of his

II

Learning to Play Backgammon

THE BEST WAY TO LEARN BACKGAMMON IS TO PLAY IT. That is true with various games, but the rule applies to backgammon more than to most other games. Due to the varied rolls of the dice, the oddities of unexpected situations, players may be forced to change tactics as they proceed, switching from one style of play to another.

In the game shown here, the moves of Black and White are shown on a numbered board, starting from the standard backgammon setup in which each player has two stones on the opposing 1–point, five stones on the opposing 12–point, three stones on his own 8–point and five stones on his own 6–point. No board is actually needed to follow the moves, as they are given in the diagrams, but it is a good idea to make the actual moves on a board, as other moves can then be tested if desired.

This is a classic game played between two competent players, with black dice representing Black's throws and white dice representing White's, though in actual play ordinary dice are used. Comments are included as to the reasons for the various moves, though many of these can be regarded as arbitrary and open to question as to whether they are the best moves.

With the board set up for play (Fig. X) White and Black each roll a single die. White's roll brings a 1 while Black comes up with a 3. Black's number being higher, he takes the opening roll, using the total shown on the two dice.

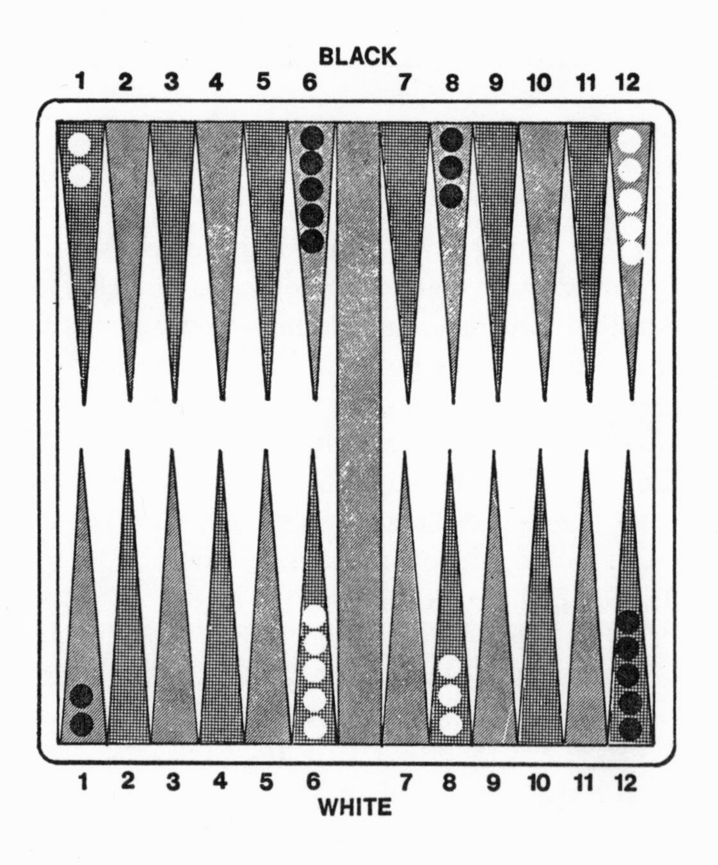

Fig. X

Black moves one stone from 8–B to 5–B and another from 6–B to 5–B. This is the standard opening and one of the best, as it enables Black to "make" his 5–point, setting up a block there.

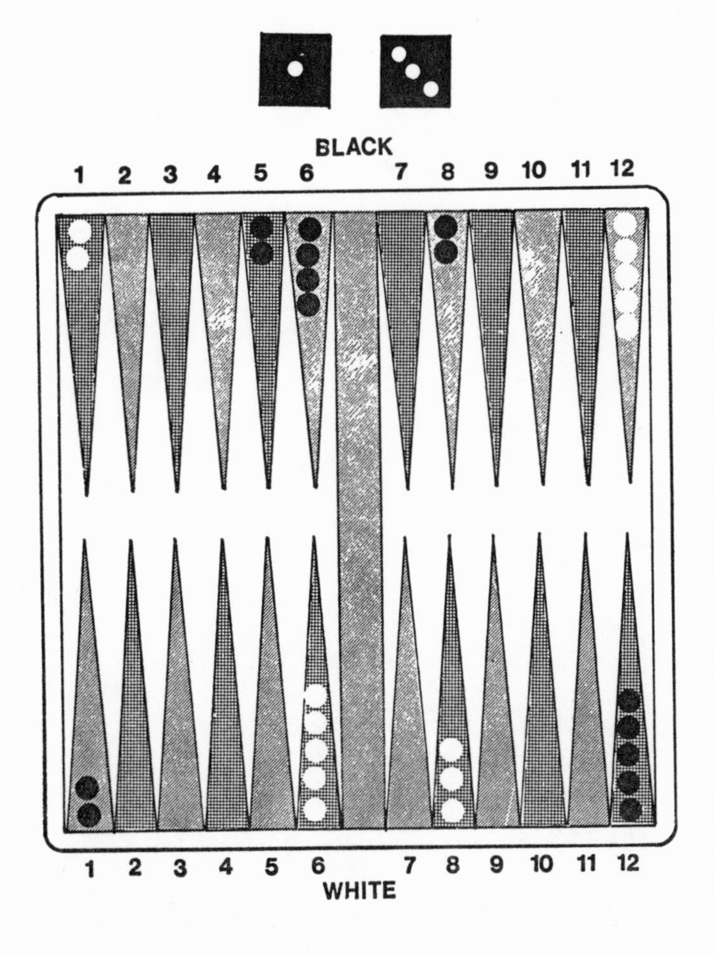

Black's roll: 3–1
(Diagram 1)

White moves from 12–B to 8–W and from 12–B to 9–W. Modern players prefer to move from 12–B to 8–W and from 1–B to 5–B; but since Black has already occupied 5–B, White has to use this substitute. A 6–1 or a 6–2 on his next roll will enable White to make his bar-point (7–W).

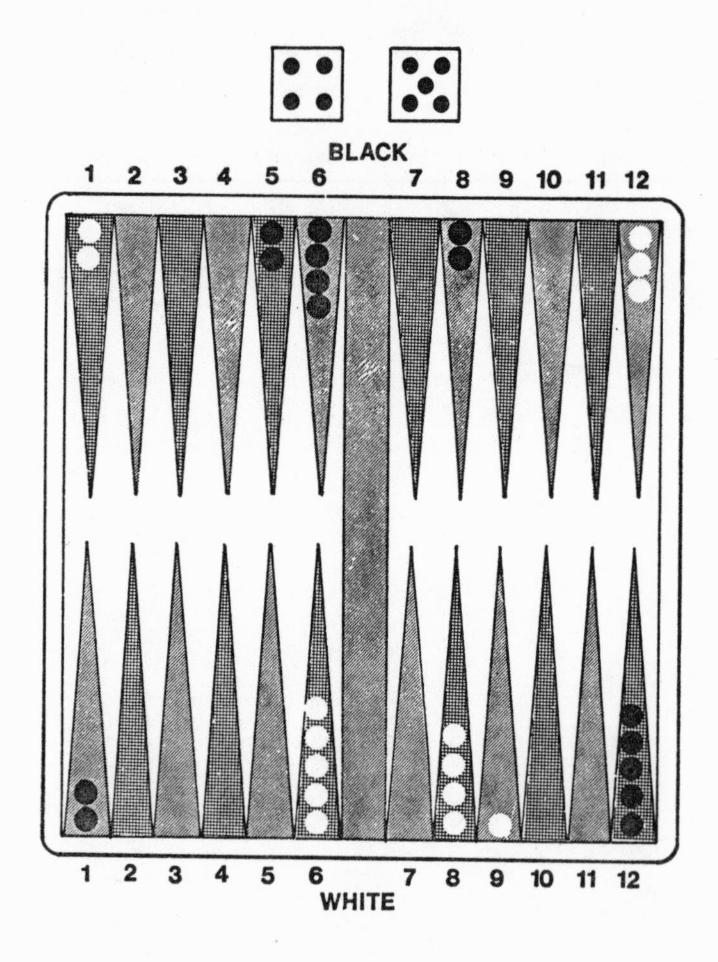

White's roll: 5–4
(Diagram 1–A)

Black usually would move both stones from 12–W to 7–B, making his bar-point and setting up four blocks in a row to confine White's back men (on 1–B and 2–B). But he sees a chance to take over White's bar-point (7–W) before White can make it, so Black moves his own back men from 1–W to 7–W, a very timely play.

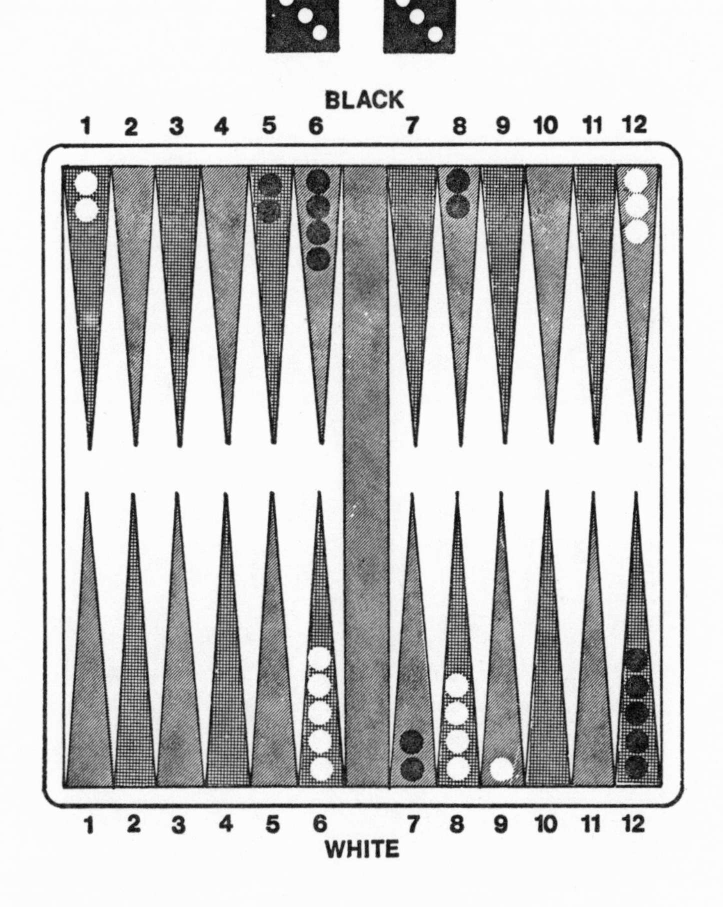

Black's roll: 3–3
(Diagram 2)

Rather than leave a blot on 9–W, White moves it to 4–W; then moves a stone from 6–W to 4–W, making his 4-point. A logical move on White's part, as it is the only point that he can make at this juncture and the block can prove valuable on 4–W, if White hits a Black blot and sends it to the bar.

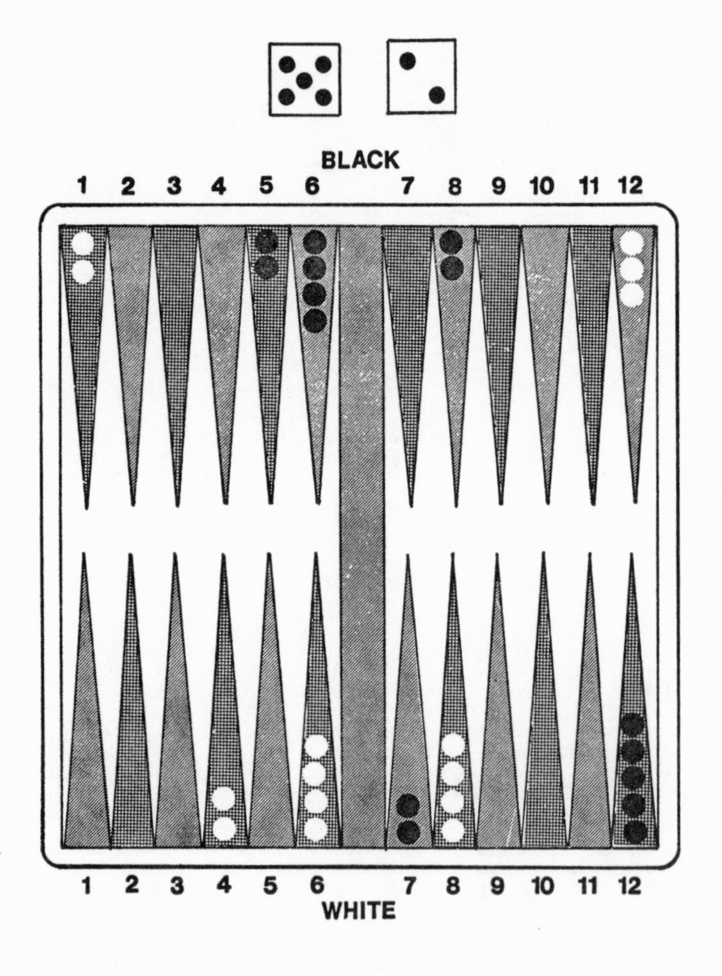

White's roll: 5–2
(Diagram 2–A)

Black moves from 12–W to 9–B, leaving one of those blots that White hopes to hit. But the risk is not great: White will have to roll a 2–6 or a 3–5 to manage it. What's more, if the Black blot is hit, Black will have a good chance of reentering it on his next roll, which is good enough.

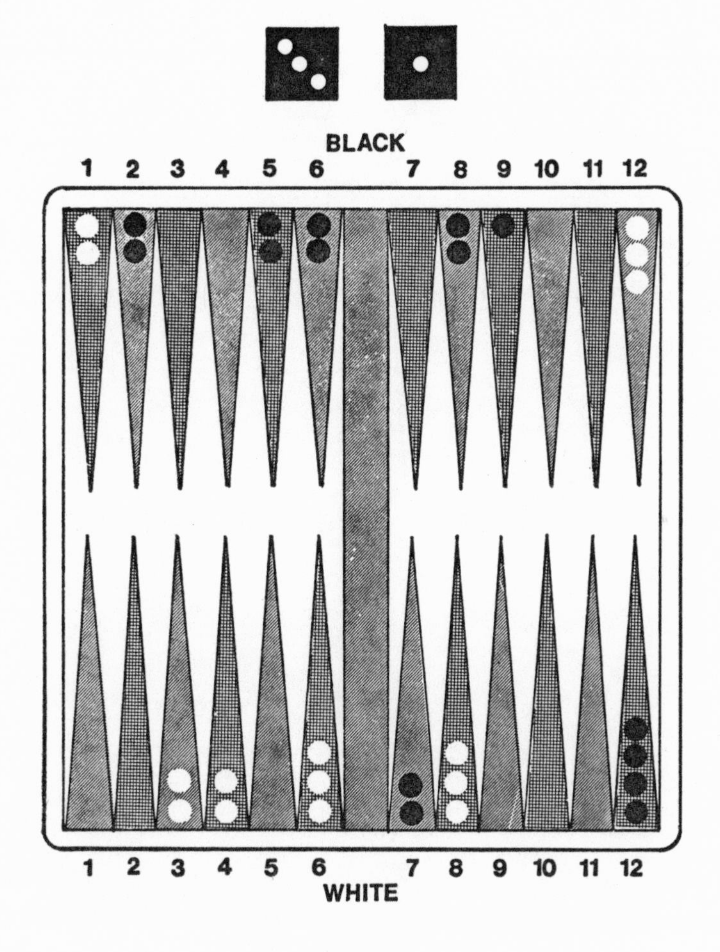

Black's roll: 3–1
(Diagram 4)

White moves from 12–B to 8–W, as another step toward the blocking game that he is concentrating on his inner table. Black's hold on White's bar-point (7–W) hasn't cramped White's style too badly; at least not so far. Maybe Black will find himself in trouble when he decides to advance those runners farther!

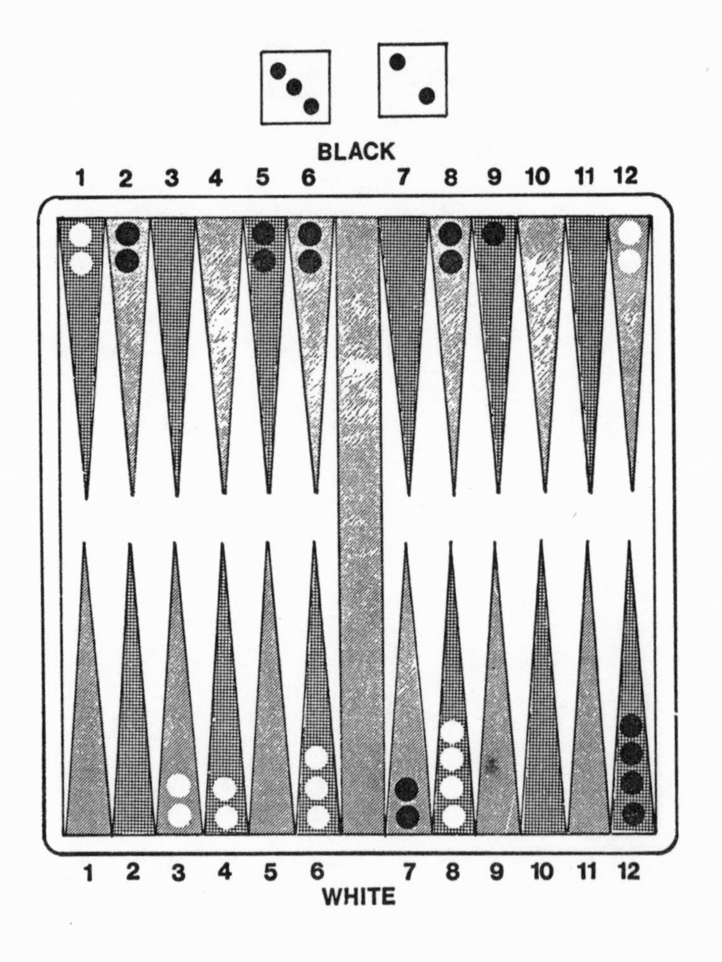

White's roll: 3–2
(Diagram 4–A)

This can be the best of rolls, not only as an opener, but almost anytime. What it lacks in power, it gains in purpose. In this case, Black handles it quite neatly. He moves his blot from 9–B to 7–B, using 1+1=2. He then moves two stones from 8–B to 7–B, putting all three on 7–B, making Black's bar-point which was hitherto neglected. Beat that, if you can!

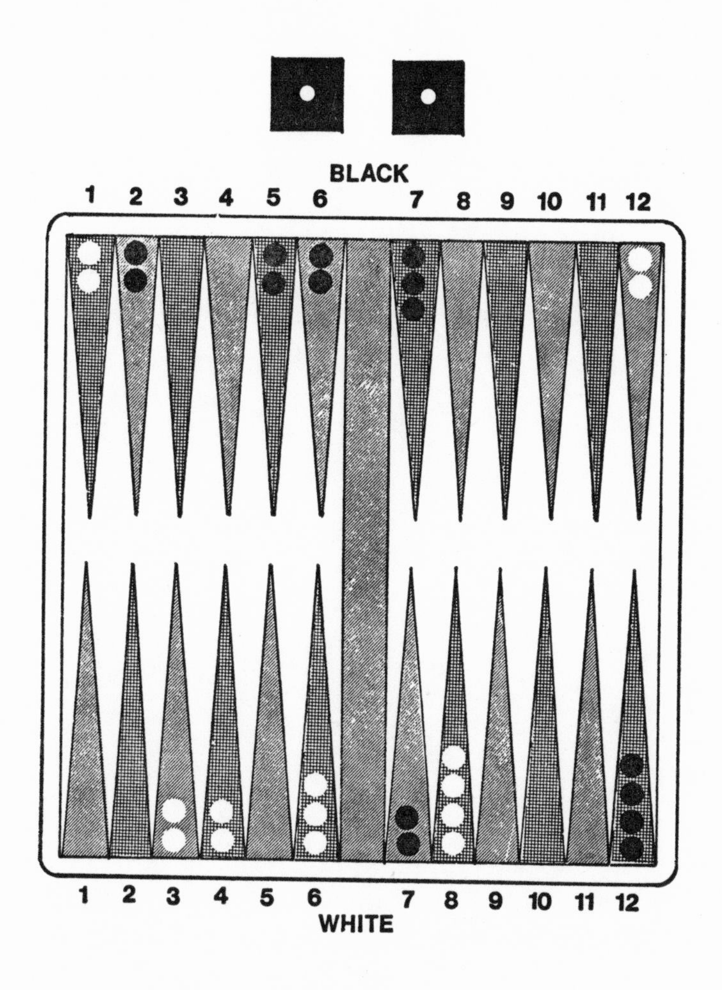

Black's roll: 1–1
(Diagram 5)

White does beat it, because it didn't worry him. He wasn't eager to hit a Black blot just now. His 4–2 roll is practically made to order. He moves one surplus stone from 8–W clear down to 2–W, where it becomes a blot that Black can't hit, because Black no longer has any back men, nor does he have a stone on the bar. Pretty nice for White.

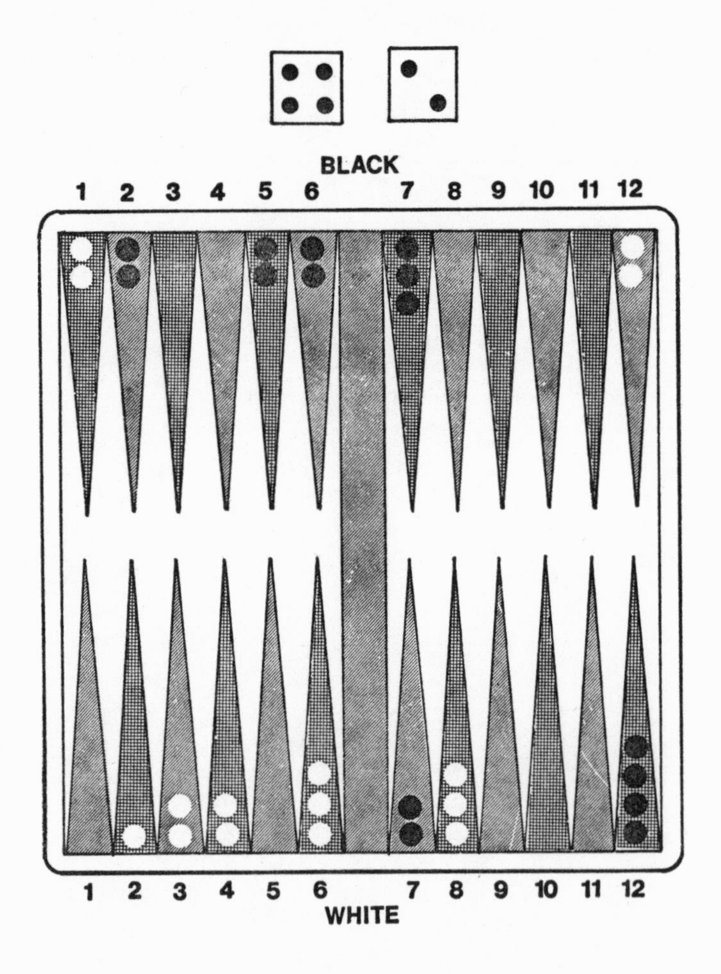

White's roll: 4–2
(Diagram 5–A)

Black repeats his previous move of 12–W to 9–B, taking the same risk with his new blot. Actually, there are only four chances out of 36 that White can roll the 2–6 or 3–5 needed to hit that Black blot. So the odds are still in Black's favor; and if White should hit the blot and send it to the bar, Black might reenter with a 2 (or 1–1), hitting White's blot on White's 2-point (2–W).

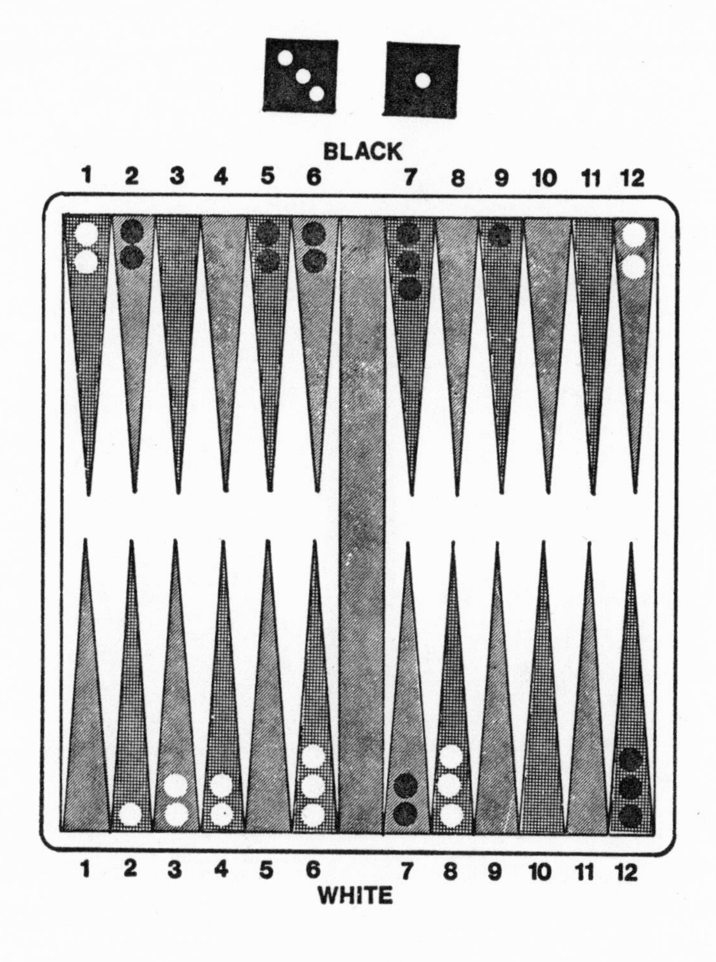

Black's roll: 3–1
(Diagram 6)

No hit by White. But he shows he is aware that Black may be inviting an exchange of blots. White moves from 8–W to 2–W, covering the stone there and making his 2–point. White is getting closer to a prime, despite those pesky Black blockers that still occupy White's coveted bar-point (7–W). That leaves only two points for reentry on White's inner table (1–W and 5–W).

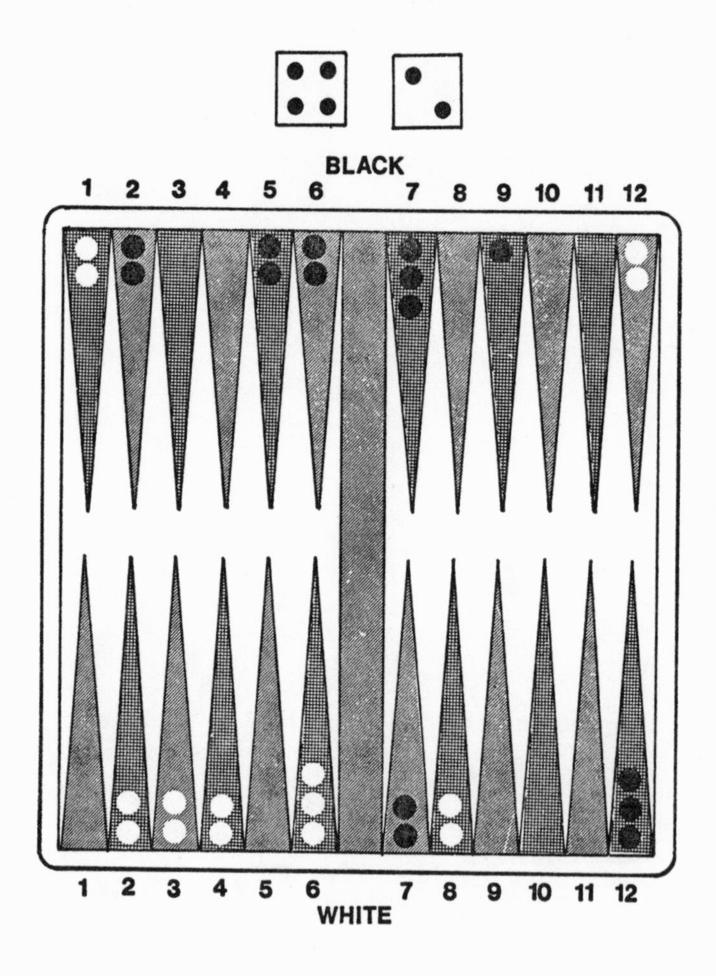

White's roll: 4–2
(Diagram 6–A)

Black gets the roll that White could have used! Now Black can end the menace by moving his blot to safety. Instead, he brings a stone from 12–W to 5–B. Apparently he hopes to keep the blot as a "builder," but White senses a deeper purpose. Black, instead of just tempting fate, may be tempting White to bring a back man from 1–B to hit the blot, thus causing White to break up his block on Black's 1-point, leaving a blot there instead.

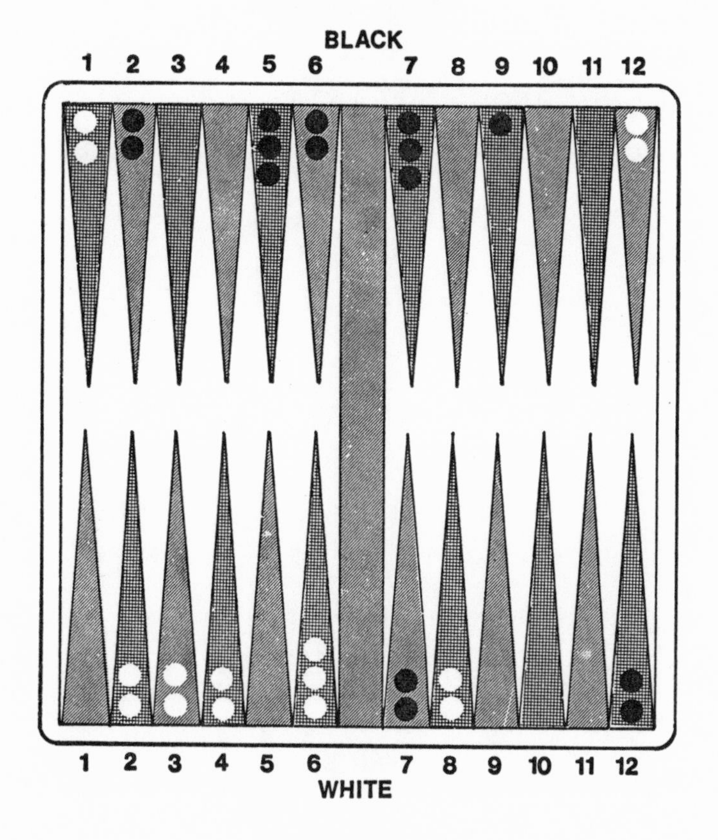

Black's roll: 6–2
(Diagram 7)

A tough break for White, rolling the biggest possible total when he can't use it to capacity. He can't move from 1–B to 7–B, nor from 12–B to 7–W, because Black holds both those bar-points. White's only move is to bring both his blockers from 8–W to 2–W, where he really doesn't want them. That uses the first half of his double 6. The other half is simply wasted.

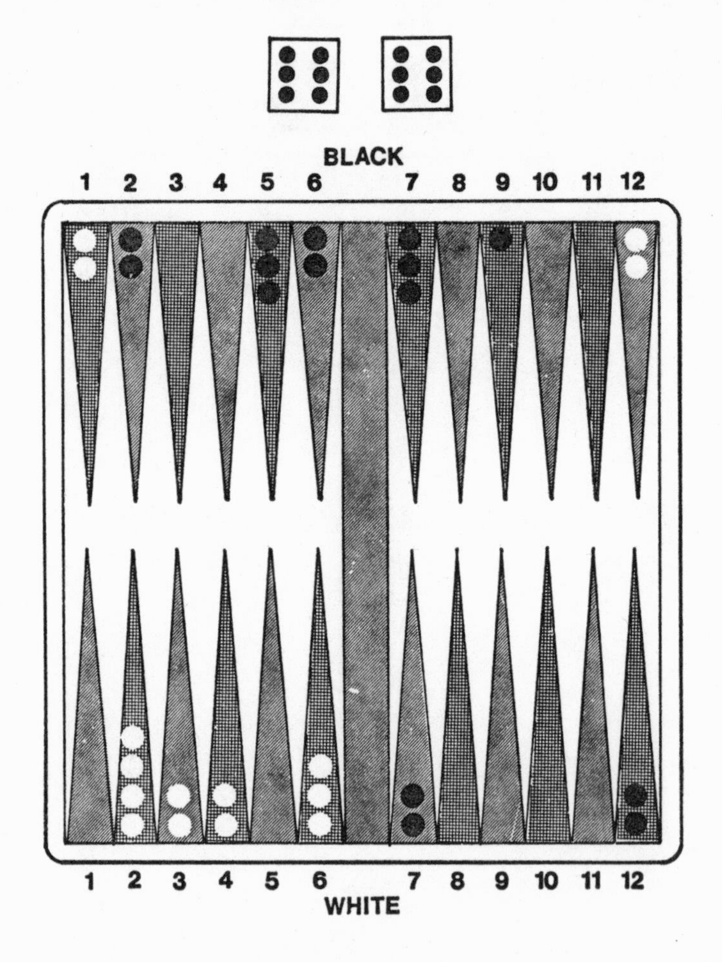

White's roll: 6–6
(Diagram 7–A)

Very neat moves for this! Black brings both stones from 12–W, using one to cover the blot on 9–B, establishing a block there and placing the other as a blot on 10–B. White can only hit the new Black blot with a roll of 3–6. That comes to only one chance in 18. The blot looks pretty safe.

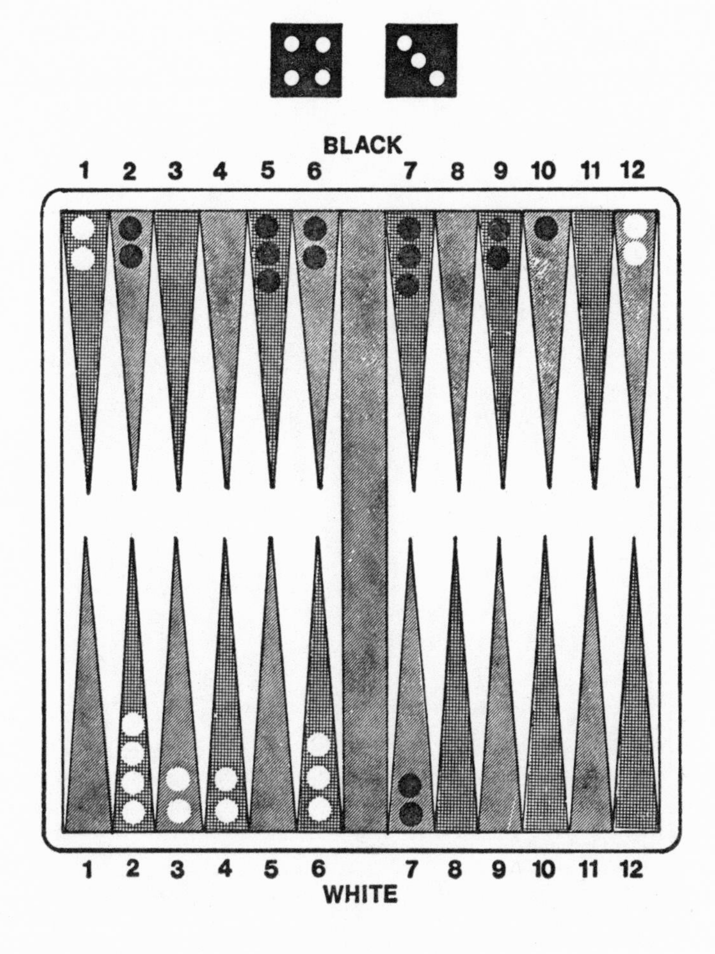

Black's roll: 4–3
(Diagram 8)

White gets the 3 but not the 6. A quick count tells him that he has a slight edge on Black, so it would be smart to bring out his runners before Black can immobilize them by establishing a prime. White moves a runner from 1–B to 4–B; then moves a surplus blocker from 2–W to 1–W as a builder toward establishing his 1–point.

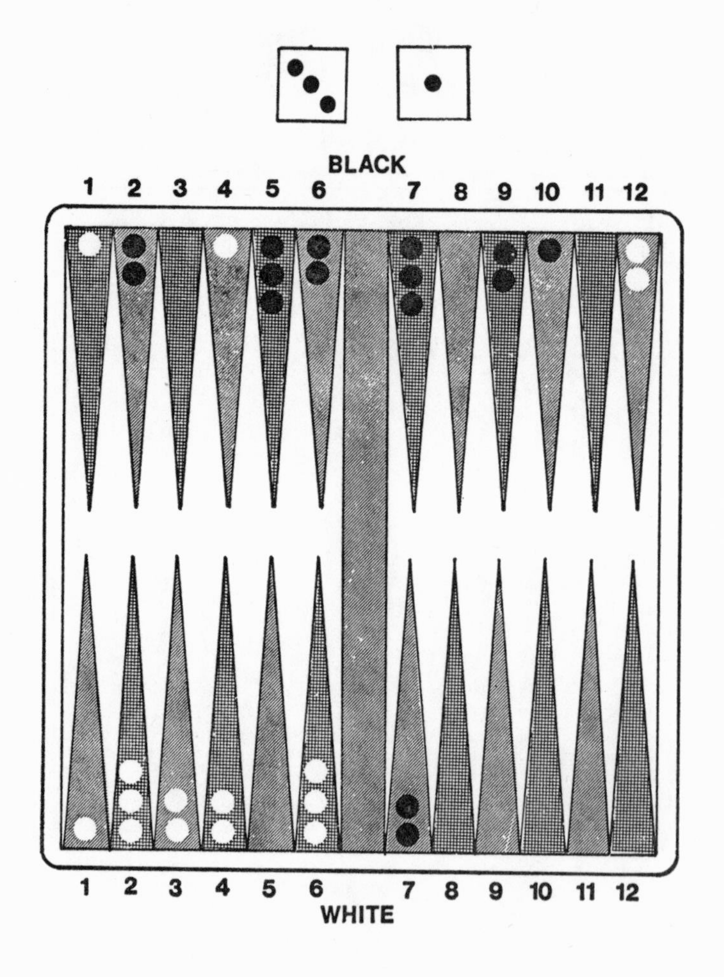

White's roll: 3–1
(Diagram 8–A)

Black moves a stone from 9–B to 4–B and another from 5–B to 4–B, hitting White's blot and sending it to the bar. At the same time, Black makes his 4–point, giving him five parts toward a prime. Things look somewhat dismal for White.

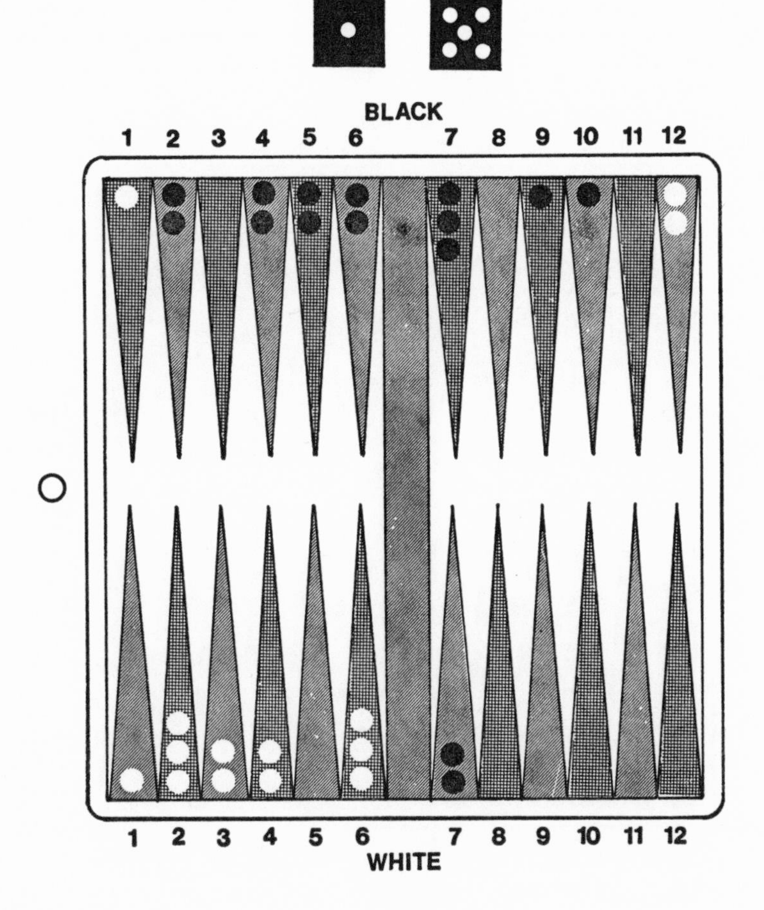

Black's roll: 1–5
(Diagram 9)

White reenters on 3–B, but is unable to move from there, as he needs a 5 or 6 to clear four Black blockers. So he moves a stone from 12–B to 9–W. This puts a White blot on each of those points, but if they are hit, White can resort to a "back game" which may help him to hit some Black blots in return.

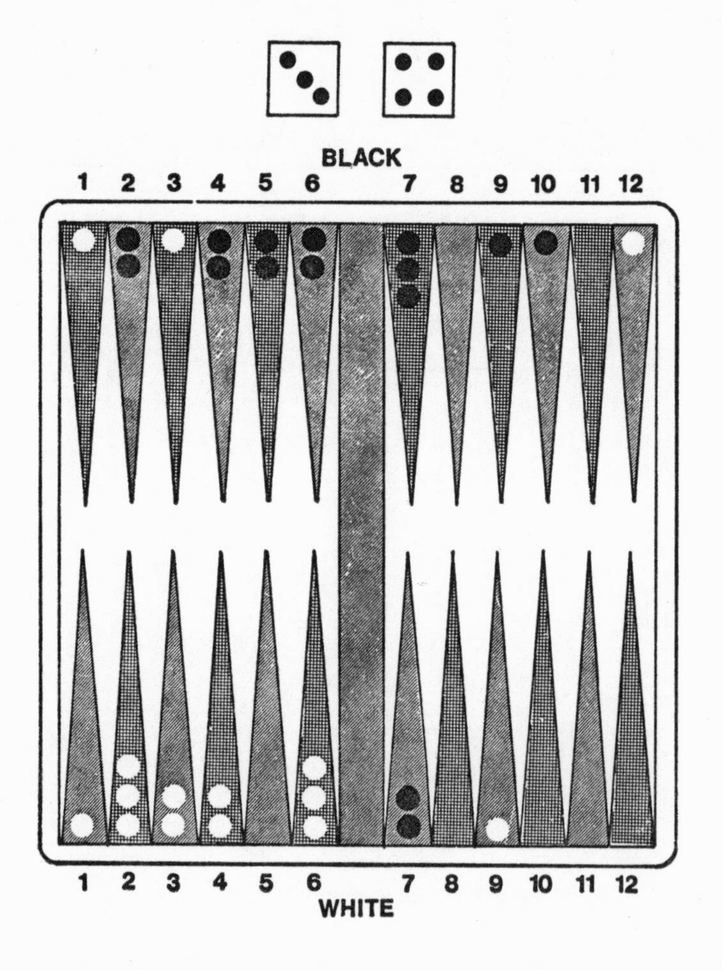

White's roll: 3–4
(Diagram 9–A)

A fine roll for Black. He moves from 7–W to 12–B, hitting the White blot and sending it to the bar. He then moves his builder from 10–B to 9–B, joining the blot already there, which gives him another block while eliminating two blots. Black's board is stronger than ever, and unless White can reenter immediately, Black may run away with things.

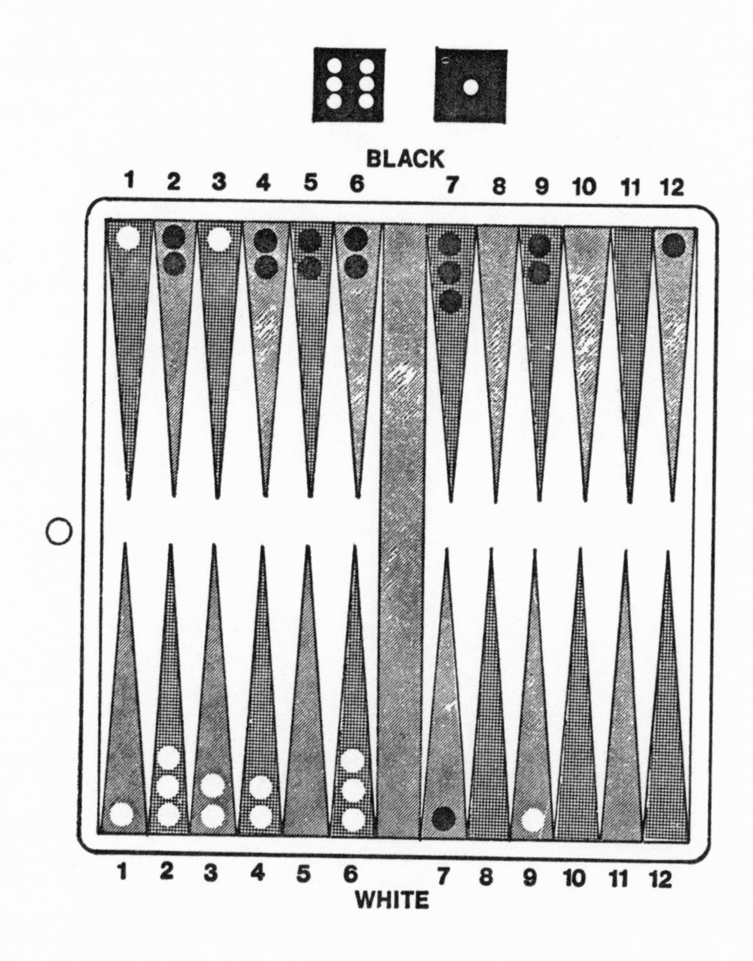

Black's roll: 6–1
(Diagram 10)

A real break for White. He enters on 3–B with his 3, establishing a block there. He then uses his 2 to move from 9–W to 7–W, hitting the Black blot on that point and sending it to the bar. White still hopes to turn his back men into runners; if that fails, he might resort to a "back game."

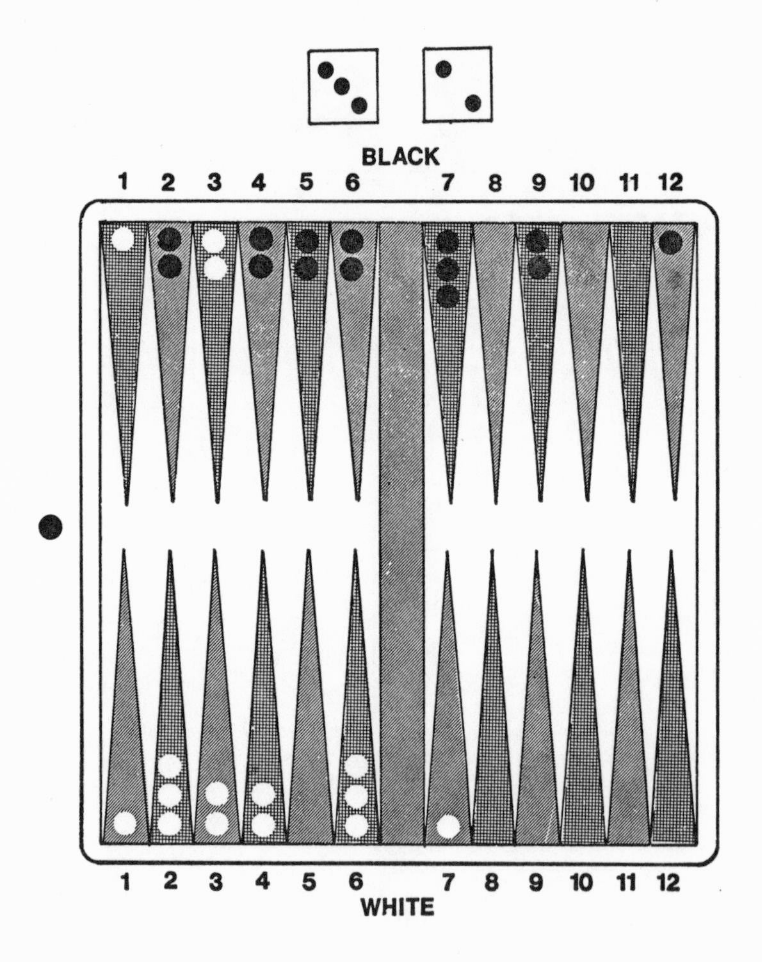

White's roll: 3–2
(Diagram 10–A)

Black enters on 1–W, hitting the blot that White unfortunately left there and sending it to the bar. Black then moves from 12–B to 9–B, eliminating his lone blot that White hoped would stay where it could be hit. About as nice a roll as Black could want at this stage of the game.

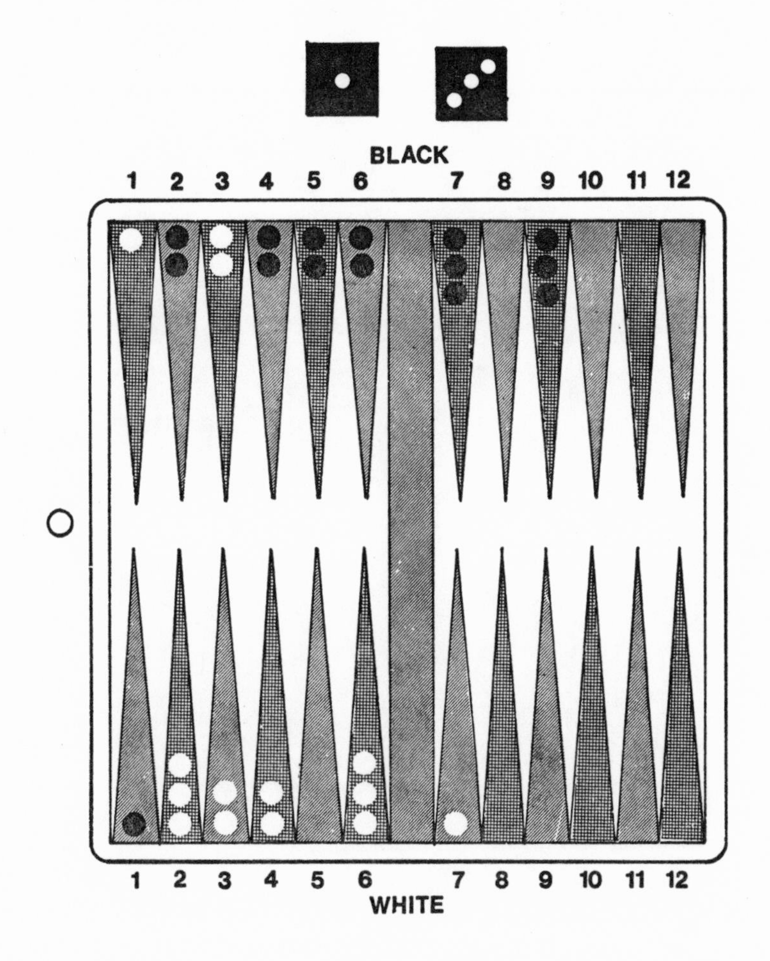

Black's roll: 1–3
(Diagram 11)

White strikes it lucky, too. He reenters on 1–B, establishing a block there; then moves one of his more advanced runners from 3–B to 8–W, hoping to get clear of Black's blockers on the next roll.

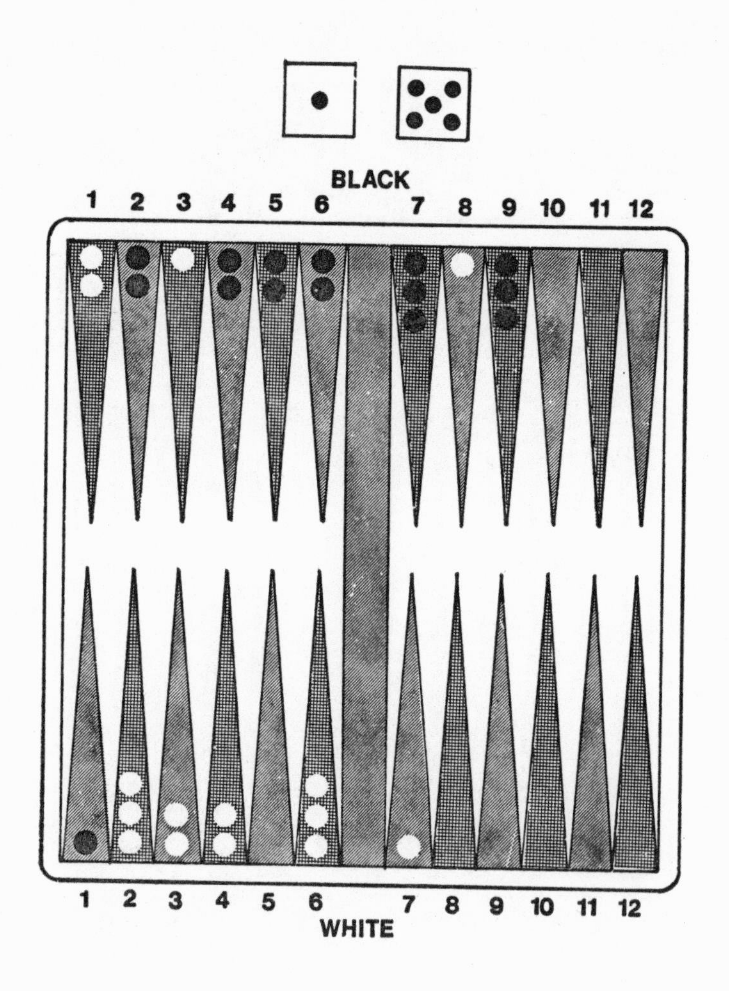

White's roll: 1–5
(Diagram 11–A)

Small though Black's roll is, it puts a damper on White's brief hope. Black moves his surplus blocker from 9–B to 8–B, hitting the White blot that just arrived there, sending it back to the bar. Black continues from 8–B to 5–B.

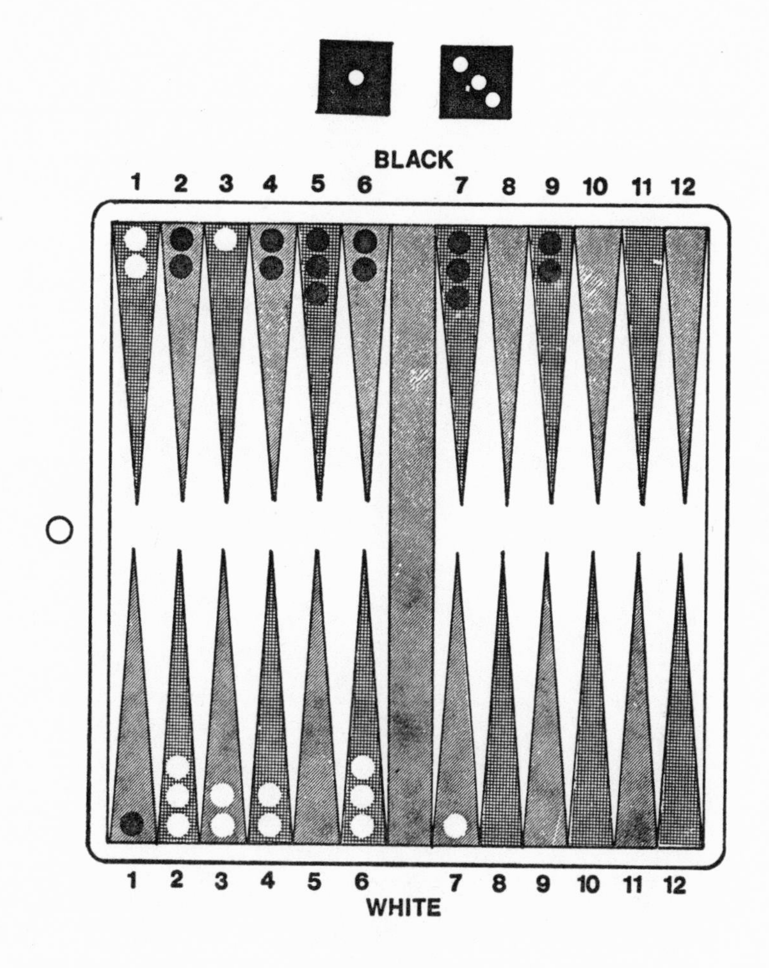

Black's roll: 1–3
(Diagram 12)

White can't reenter his stone from the bar, hence he can't move any of the others, so his roll is wasted. That's too bad, as the 2 would have enabled him to move one runner from 1–B to 3–B, getting that much closer to freedom.

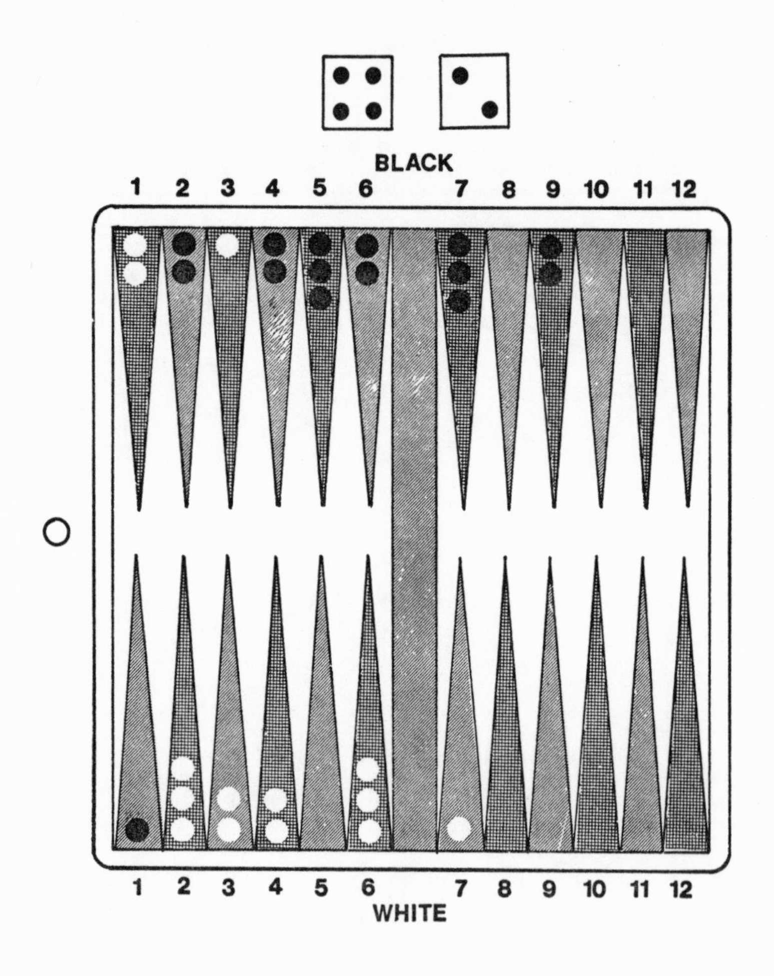

White's roll: 4–2
(Diagram 12–A)

Black, by using his 4 first, brings his runner from 1–W to 5–W and from there to 10–W, which, oddly, is better than hitting the White blot on 7–W. If White had another stone on the bar, it could prove helpful toward a "back game" which may soon be White's only hope.

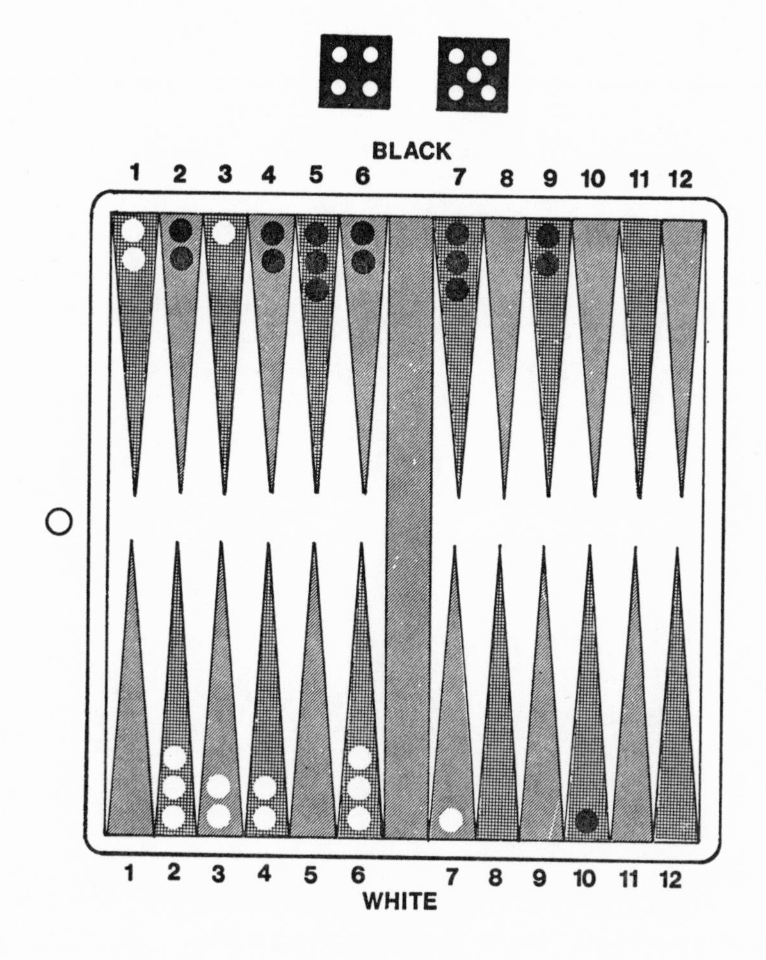

Black's roll: 4–5
(Diagram 13)

Again, White can not reenter, so must waste a move. which in this case would have enabled his runner on 3–B to wing far on his way to freedom (by treating the roll as 5–6). Just another dash of frustration for White.

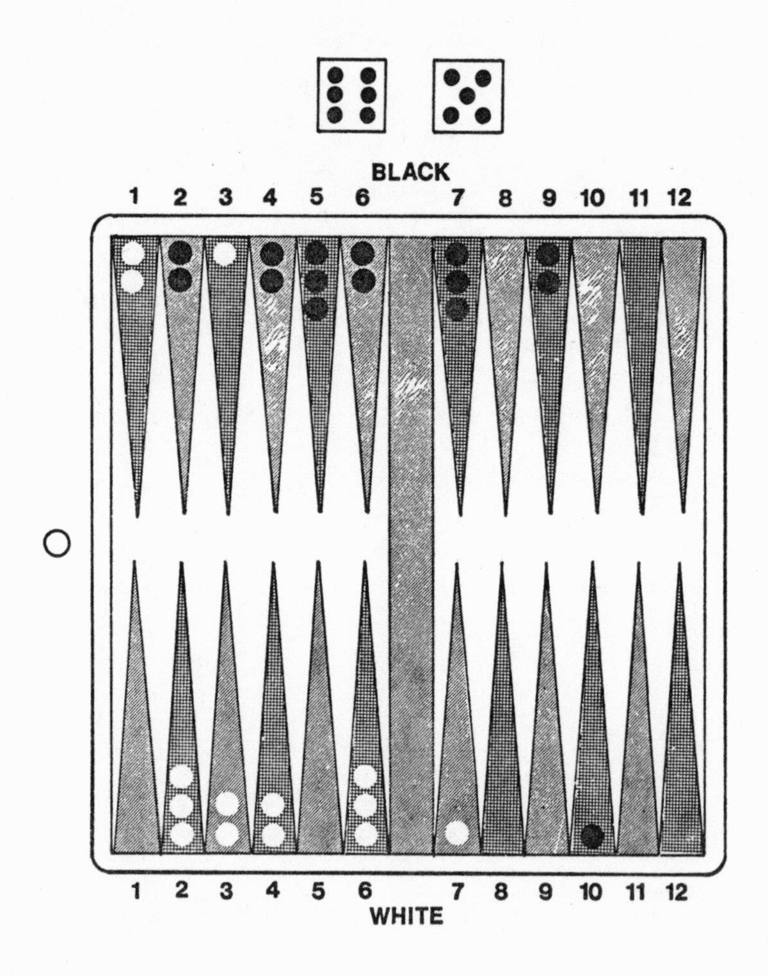

White's roll: 6–5
(Diagram 13–A)

Black brings his runner clear from 10–W to 6–B. In three more moves, Black hopes to have all his stones on his inner table (points 1 to 6 inclusive) and from there he can begin to "bear off."

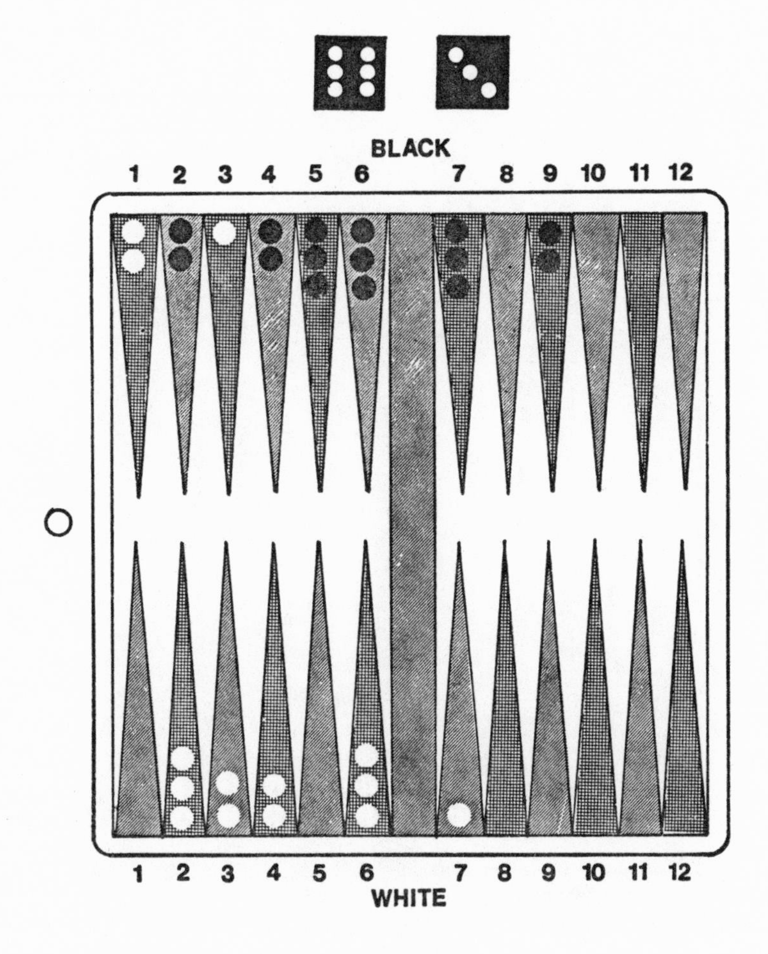

Black's roll: 6–3
(Diagram 14)

A big help for White! He enters his stranded stone on 1–B; then moves his blot from 7–W to 5–W (1+1) and finally moves the surplus blocker from 6–W to 5–W. This gives White 5 points toward a prime on his inner table, which could have been a big help earlier, but now may be too late.

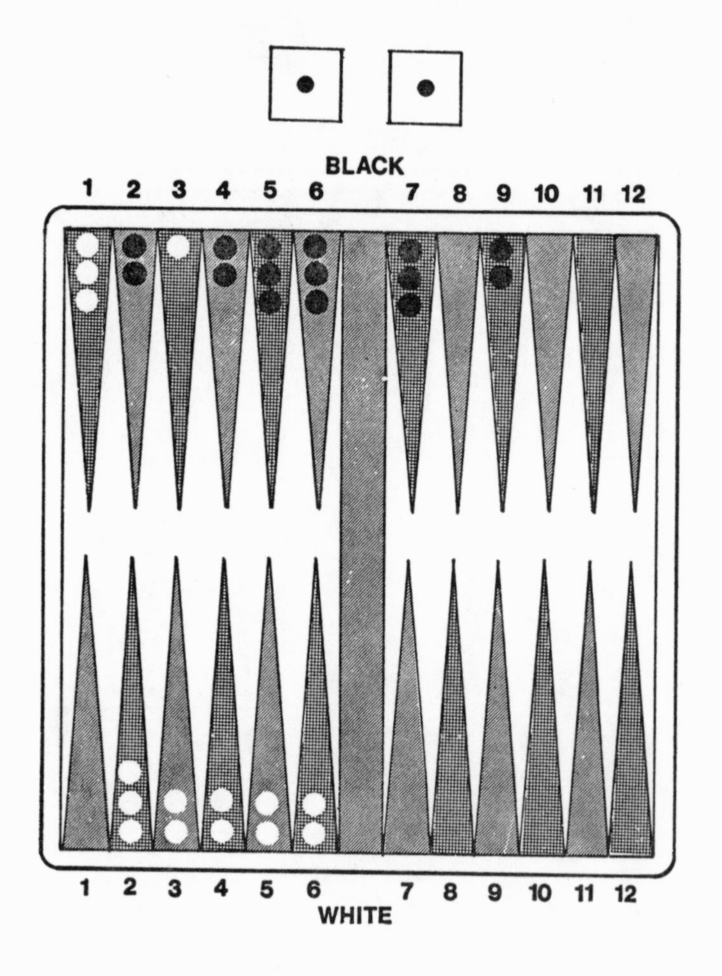

White's roll: 1–1
(Diagram 14–A)

Black is getting everything his way. He moves one of his blockers from 9–B to 3–B and another from 7–B to 3–B, hitting the white blot and sending it to the bar. With it, Black makes his "prime" of 6 points in a row, so that even if White does get off the bar, he can't turn his back men into runners, because Black has hemmed them in completely.

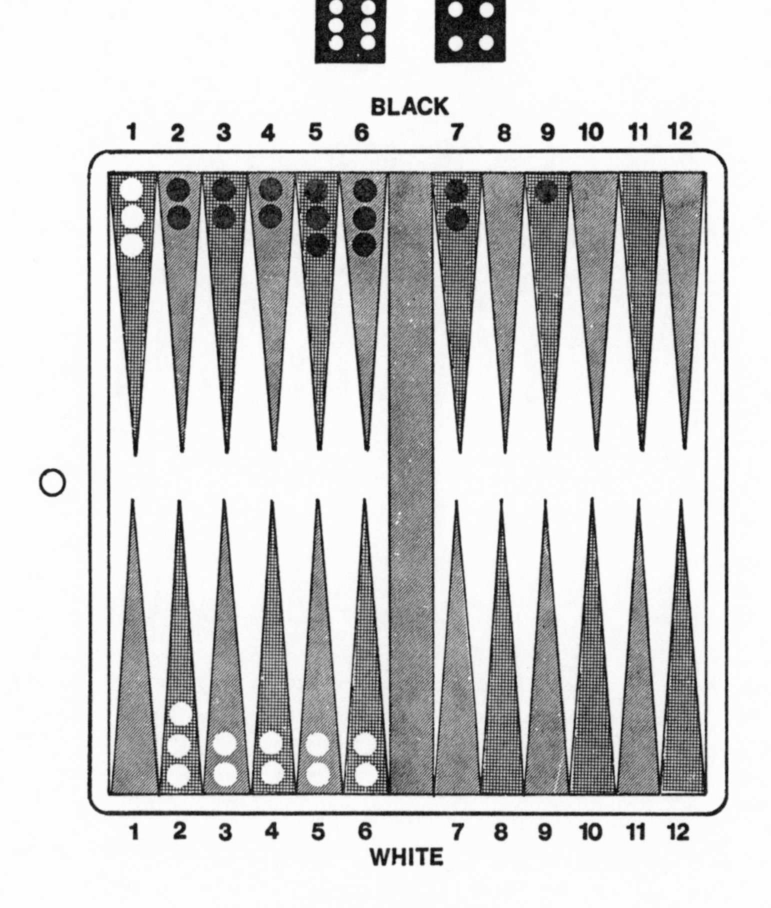

Black's roll: 6–4
(Diagram 15)

Again, a 1–1 puts White back in play. He reenters on 1–B and simply moves his three blockers from 2–W to 1–W (1+1+1) which is just as good as having them on 2–W as White still holds 5 points on his inner table. But he can't hope to hold them very long!

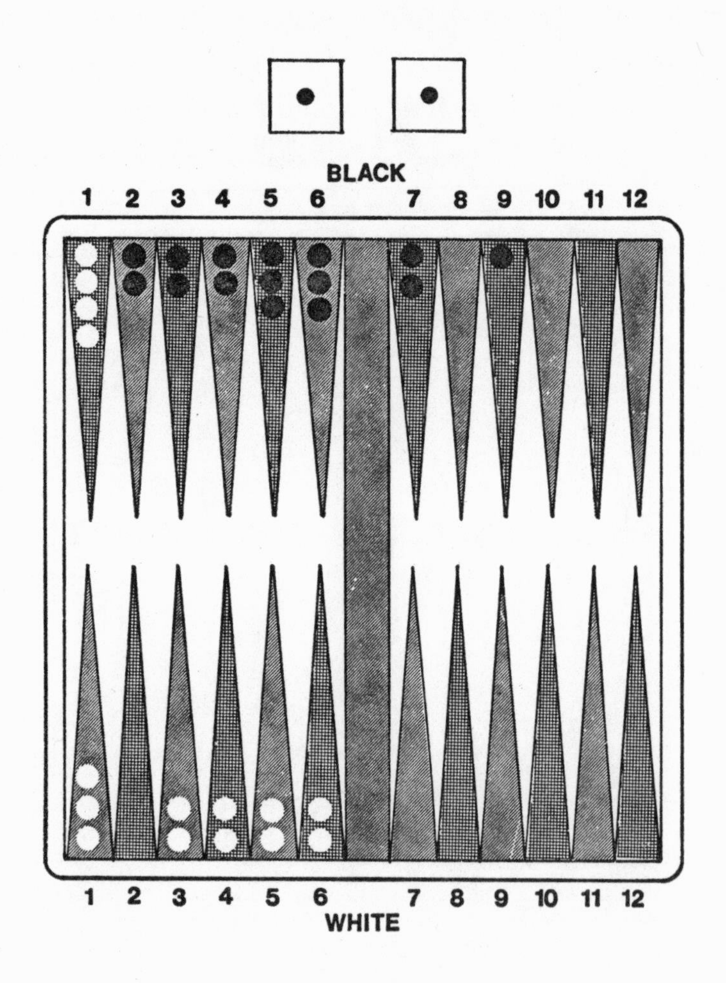

White's roll: 1–1
(Diagram 15–A)

Here, a big roll really boomerangs on Black, forcing him to move his blot from 9–B to 3–B and a blocker from 7 B to 2 B. This ruins Black's prime and forces him to leave a blot where White can hit it. Now, Black is jittery. Remembering that White rolled 1–1 twice in a row, he realizes that a roll of 6–6 could free all of White's back men and put White on the way to a win, since Black's blot would be hit and sent to the bar!

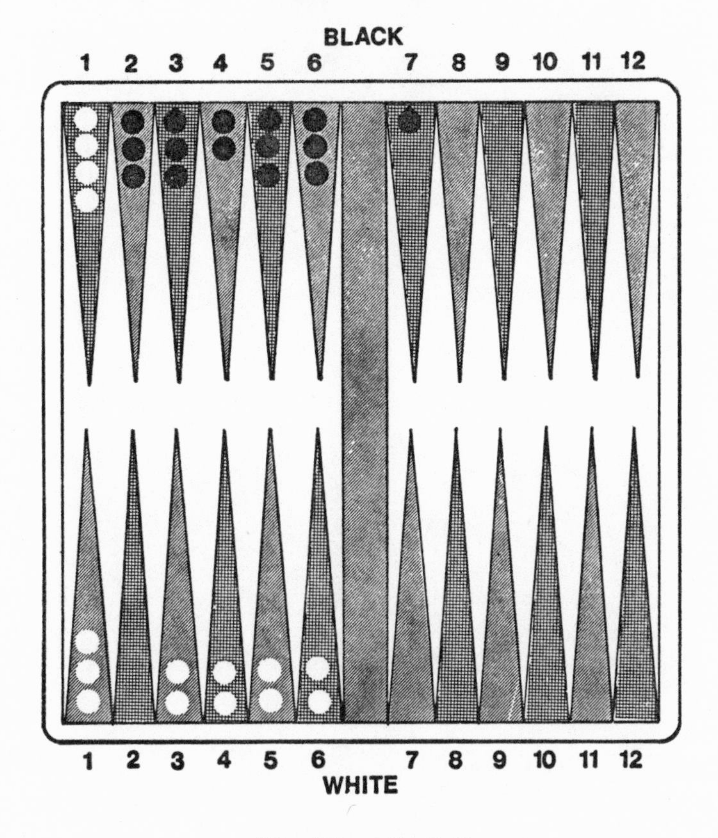

Black's roll: 6–5
(Diagram 16)

Small though this roll is, it weakens White badly. forcing him to move from 4–W to 1–W and from 4–W to 2–W. He now has only 4 points covered on his inner table and he is forced to leave a blot on his 2 point (2–W) though that can hardly matter at the moment.

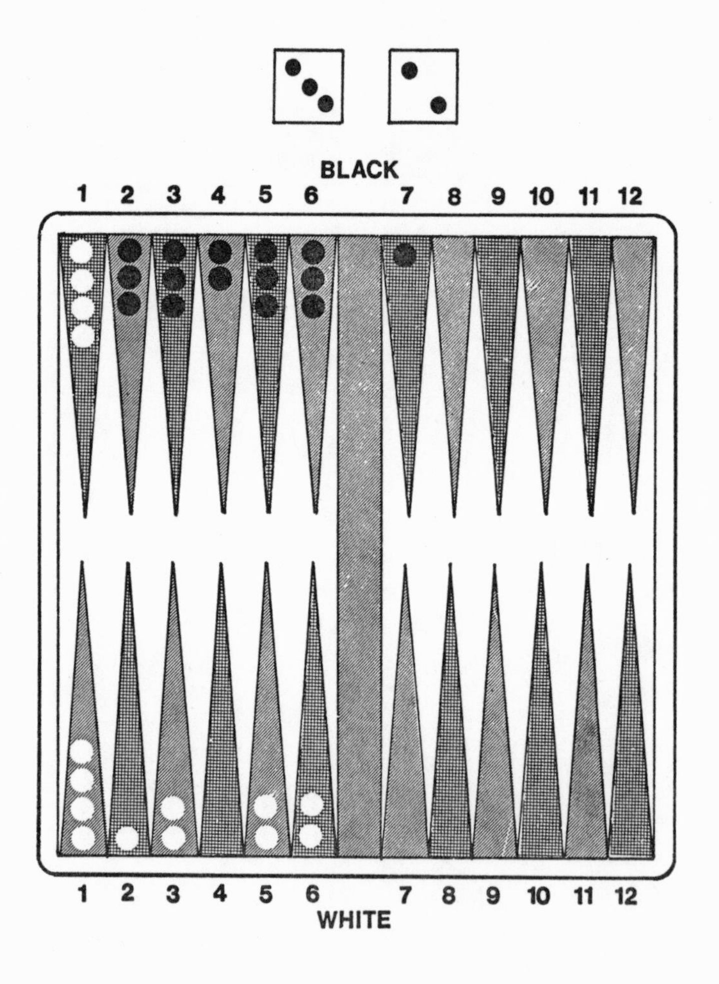

White's roll: 3–2
(Diagram 16–A)

Note that Black puts the 3 ahead of the 6. This enables Black to move his blot from 7–B to 4–B, getting all his stones on his inner table. He then "bears off" a stone from 6–B. Oddly, a 6–6 would have been the worst possible roll for Black, as he couldn't have moved his blot from 7–B and would have had to leave it there for White to hit. In short, Black would have wasted a 6–6 entirely.

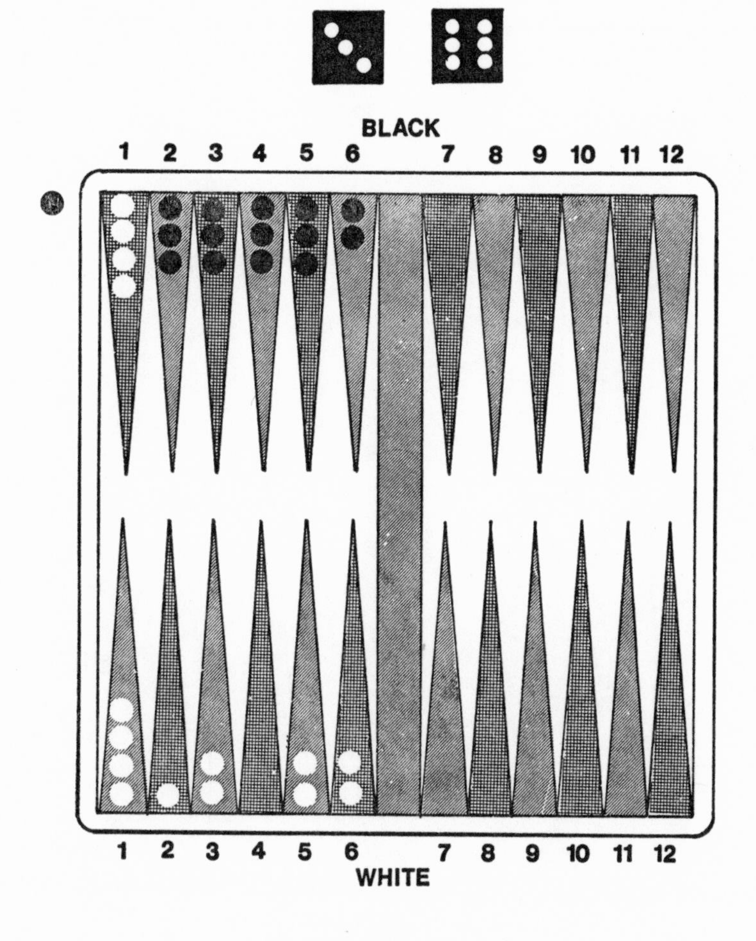

Black's roll: 3–6
(Diagram 17)

White moves two stones from 6–W to 2–W and two from 5–W to 1–W. White now has only 3 points covered on his inner table. A roll of 6–6 could still turn all his back men into runners, but he would need a few more big doubles in succession to catch up with Black, who is due to bear off further.

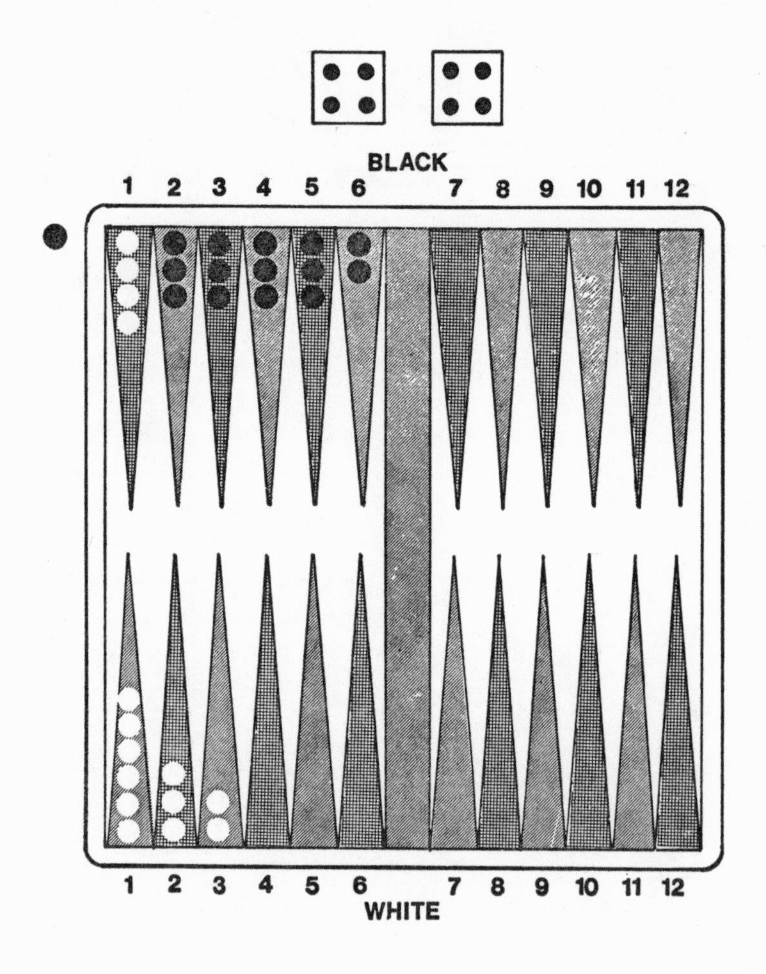

White's roll: 4–4
(Diagram 17–A)

Black bears off a stone from 4–B and moves another from 3–B to 2–B. This keeps his blocks intact, though of course his bar-point (7–B) is still open. Black's only worry is that as he continues to bear off, he will be forced to leave blots that White's back men can hit and send to the bar. That would prevent Black from bearing off further until he can reenter such stones and bring them clear around to his inner table.

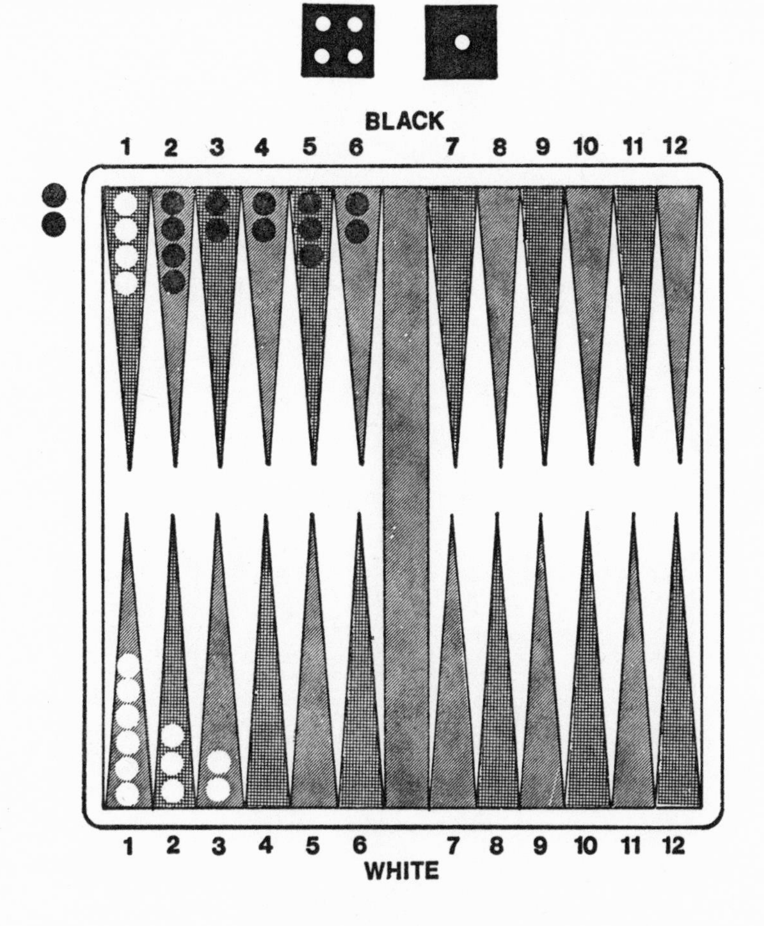

Black's roll: 4–1
(Diagram 18)

White moves from 3–W to 1–W and from 3–W to 2–W. Even this small roll hurts White's cause by reducing his coverage to two points on his inner table (1–W and 2–W). White now must resort to a form of "back game," which consists of hitting opposing blots as they occur and hitting them again after they reenter.

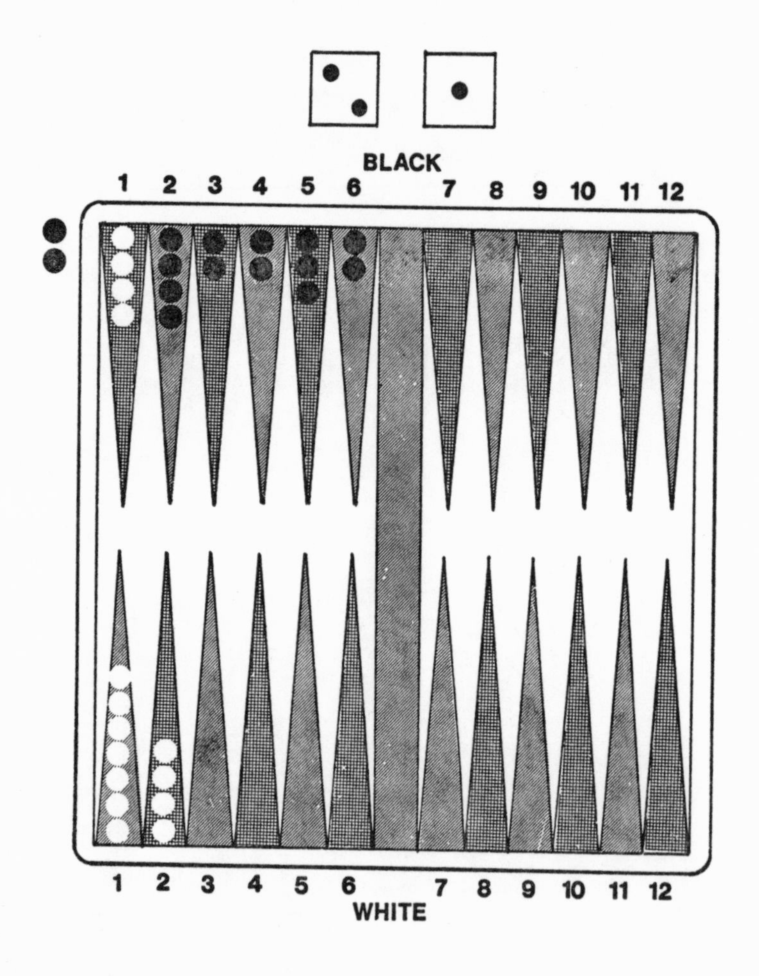

White's roll: 2–1
(Diagram 18–A)

Black bears off from 4–B and also from 2–B. This leaves a blot on 4–B, but if White should hit it, Black could easily reenter. Black could have moved from 6–B to 2–B and from 6–B to 4–B instead of bearing off, but he apparently felt that he was far enough ahead to risk the blot.

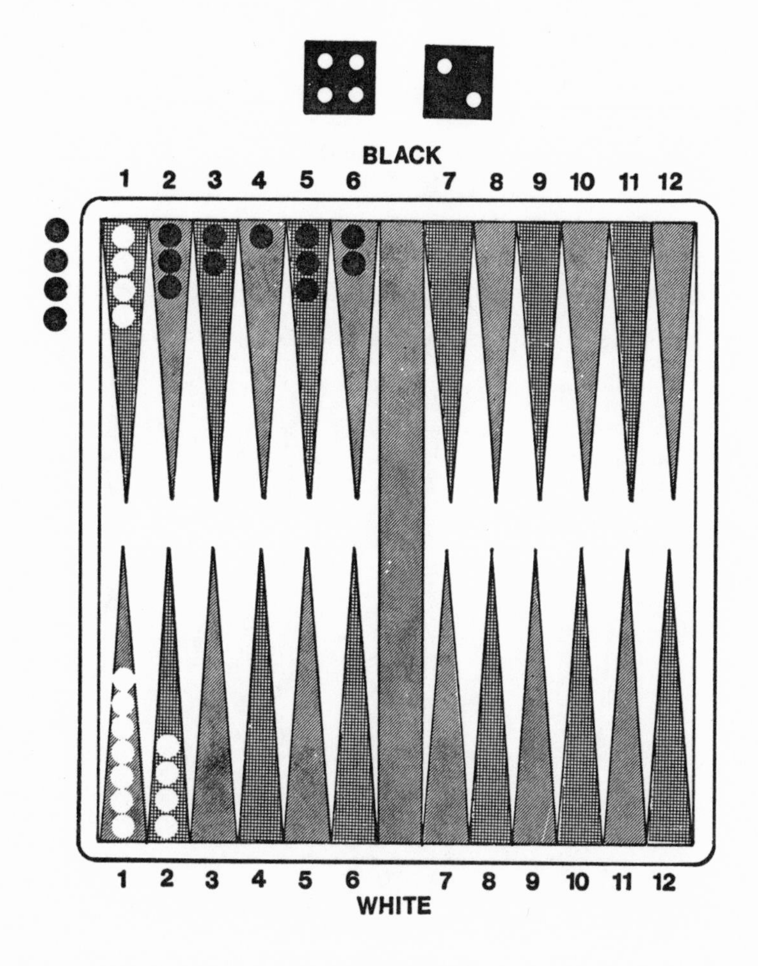

Black's Roll: 4–2
(Diagram 19)

White moves a runner from 1–B to 12–B. Using the conventional opening move at this late stage is purely coincidental, as no other move is possible for White. Again, a 6–6 was the roll that White really needed here.

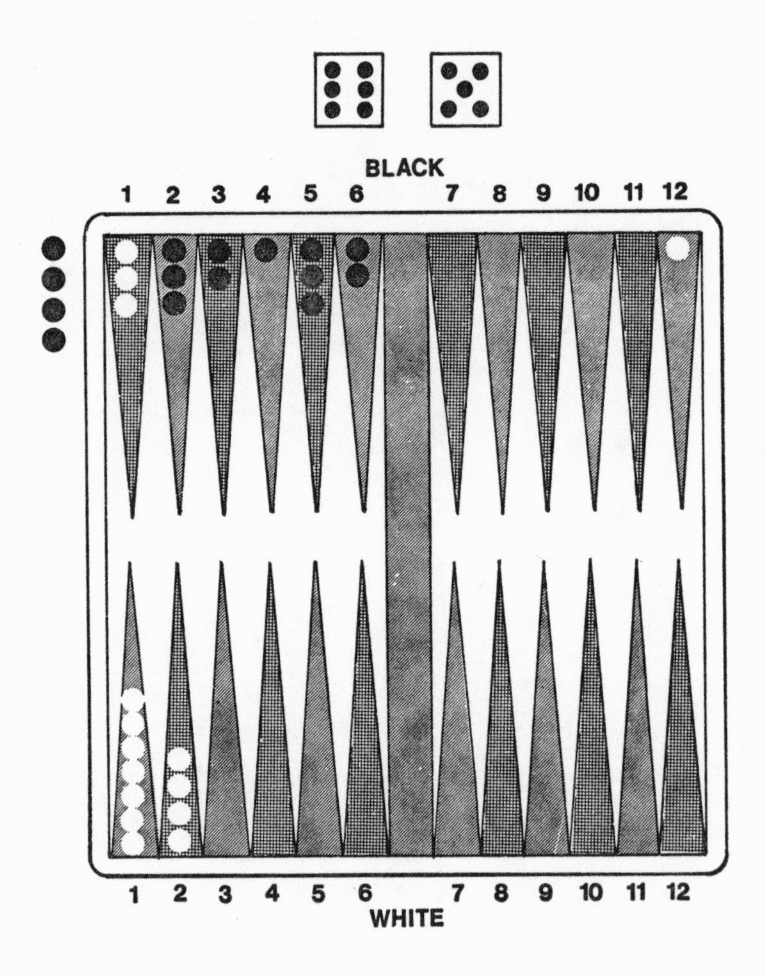

White's roll: 6–5
(Diagram 19–A)

Black bears off from 5–B and from 4–B, thus disposing of his only blot. Black still has blocks on four points of his inner table, so things are still tough for White. Black hopes to finish bearing off in five rolls of the dice.

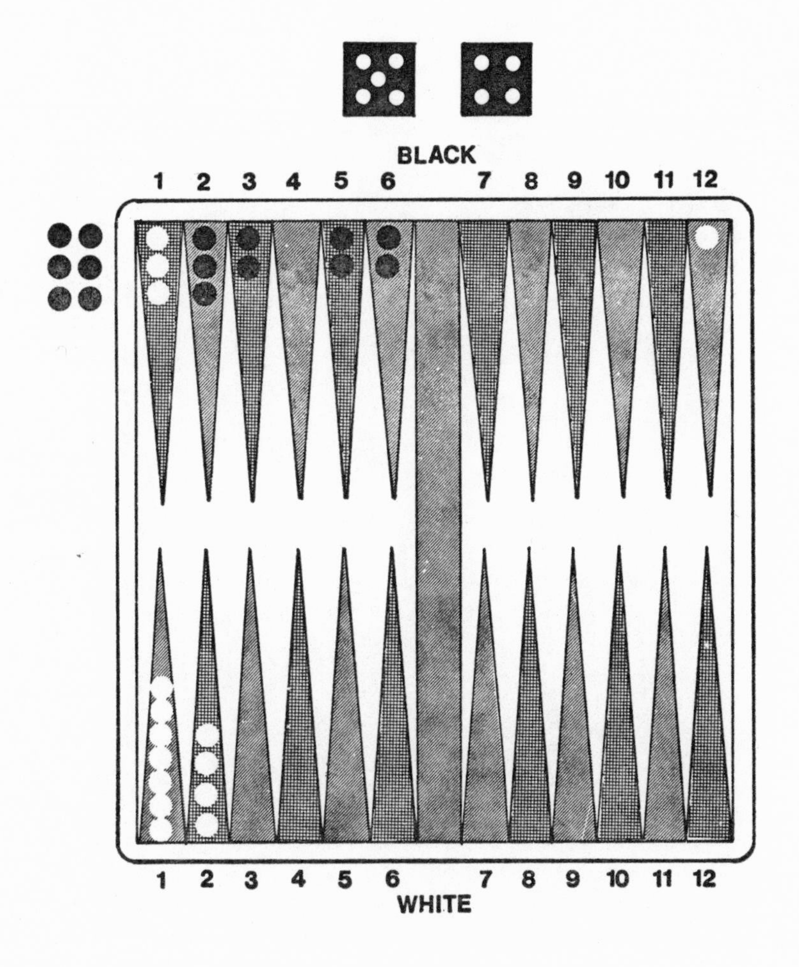

Black's roll: 5–4
(Diagram 20)

White's only possible move is from 12–B to W–7, so he makes it. White is still hoping for a chance to hit a Black blot with one of his three back men.

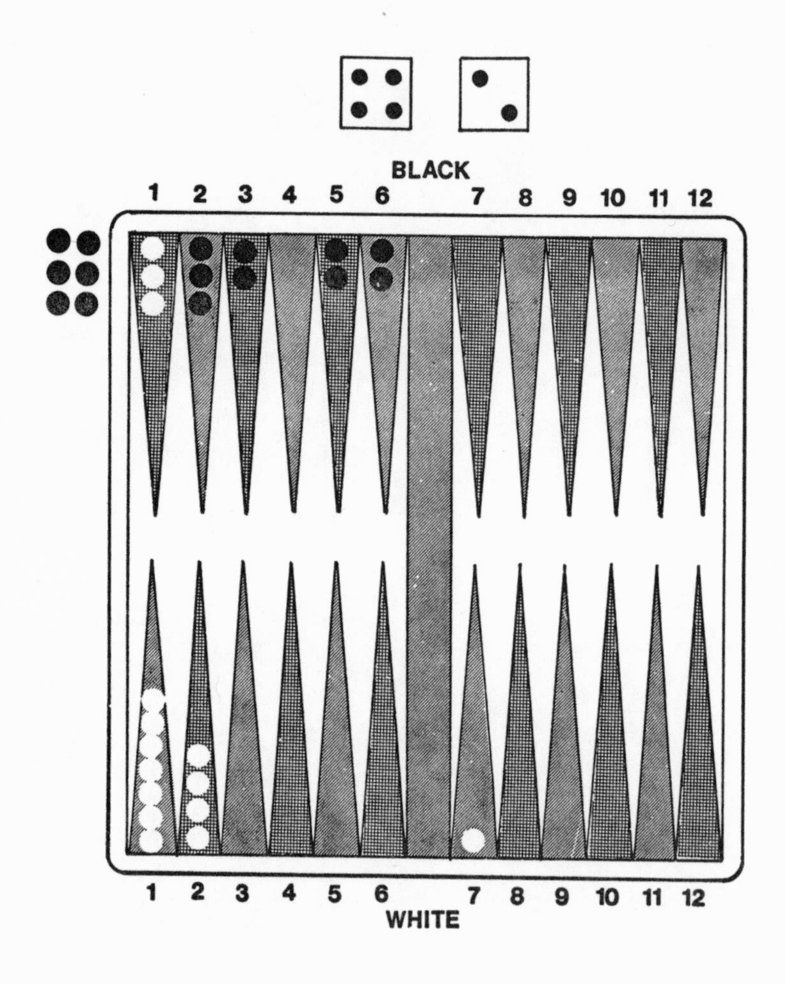

White's roll: 4–2
(Diagram 20–A)

Black bears off from 6–B and moves from 6–B to 3–B, but leaves no blot for White to hit. However, Black opens his 6–point, giving White a better chance to advance another runner. Black hopes to bear off all his stones in four more rolls.

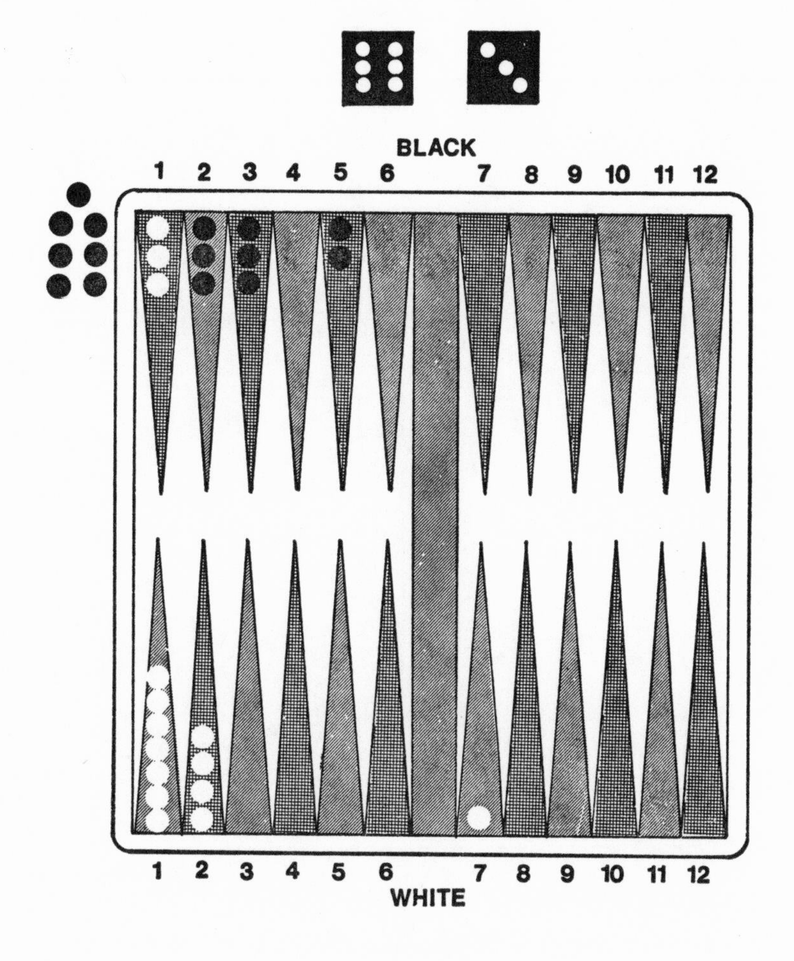

Black's roll: 6–3
(Diagram 21)

White moves a runner from 1–B to 8–B. If White's forthcoming rolls average a total of eight each, it will take six rolls for him to bring all his runners to his inner table. White needs a better break than that to avoid being "gammoned."

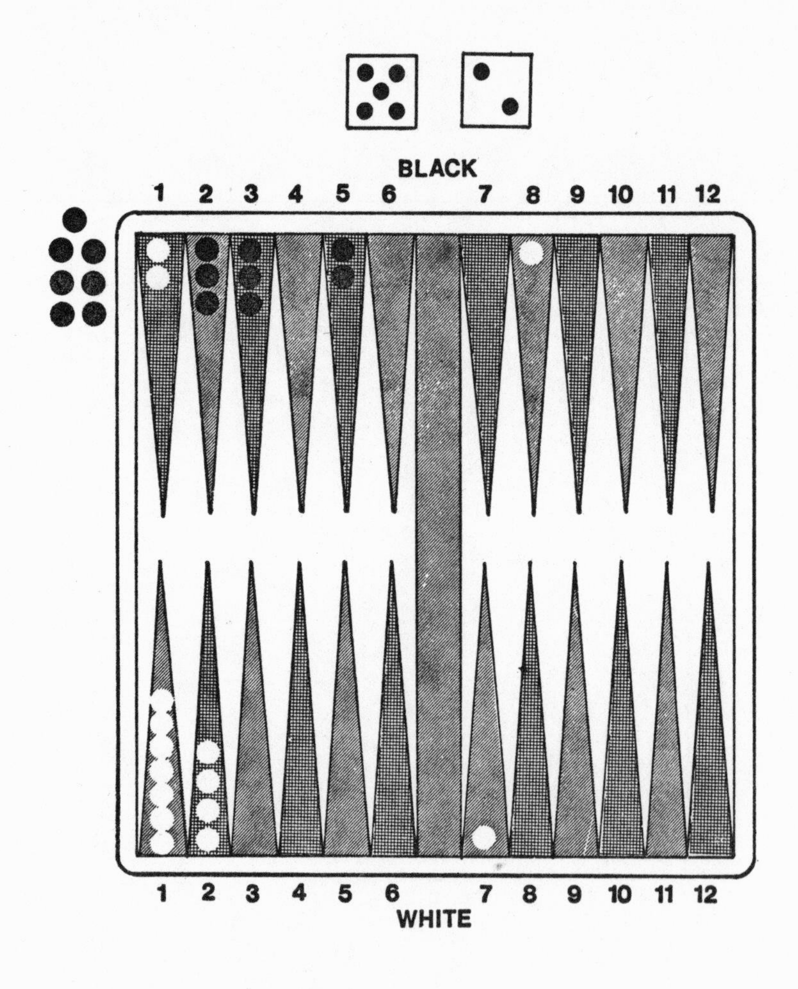

White's roll: 5–2
(Diagram 21–A)

Black has to use his 6 to bear off from 5–B, but he is unable to use his 4 to move from 5–B to 1–B, because White has that point blocked. Not only does this slow Black's process of bearing off; it forces him to leave a blot on 5–B, giving White a chance to hit it.

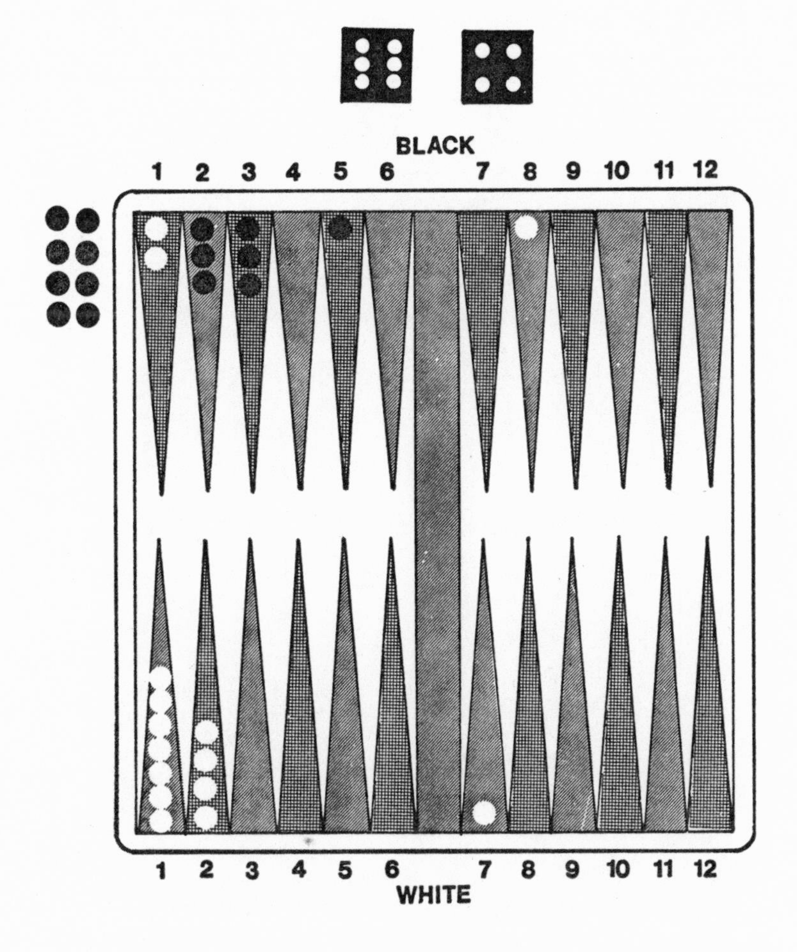

Black's roll: 6–4
(Diagram 22)

White fails to roll the needed 4 that would enable him to hit Black's blot. So he moves from 8–B to 9–W, keeping his back men on 1–B, hoping they can still hit that Black blot—and perhaps another.

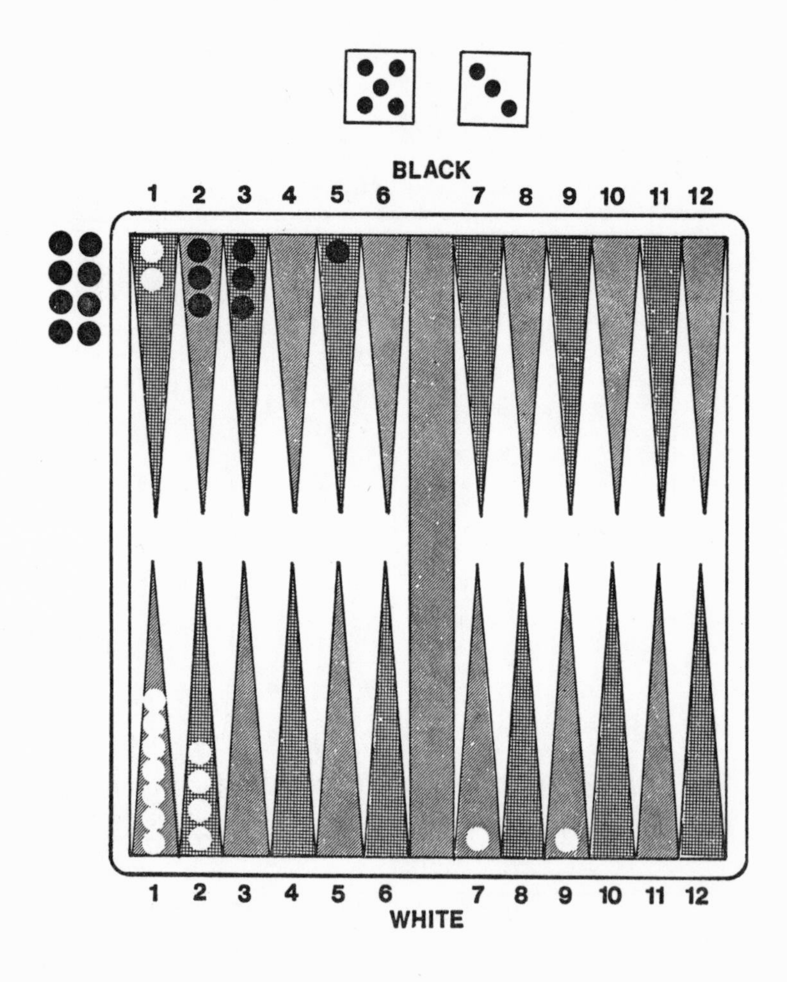

White's roll: 5–3
(Diagram 22–A)

Black bears off from 5–B, but is unable to bear off another stone, so has to settle with a move from 3–B to 2–B. However, he gets rid of the blot on 5–B, so the situation becomes tougher than ever for White.

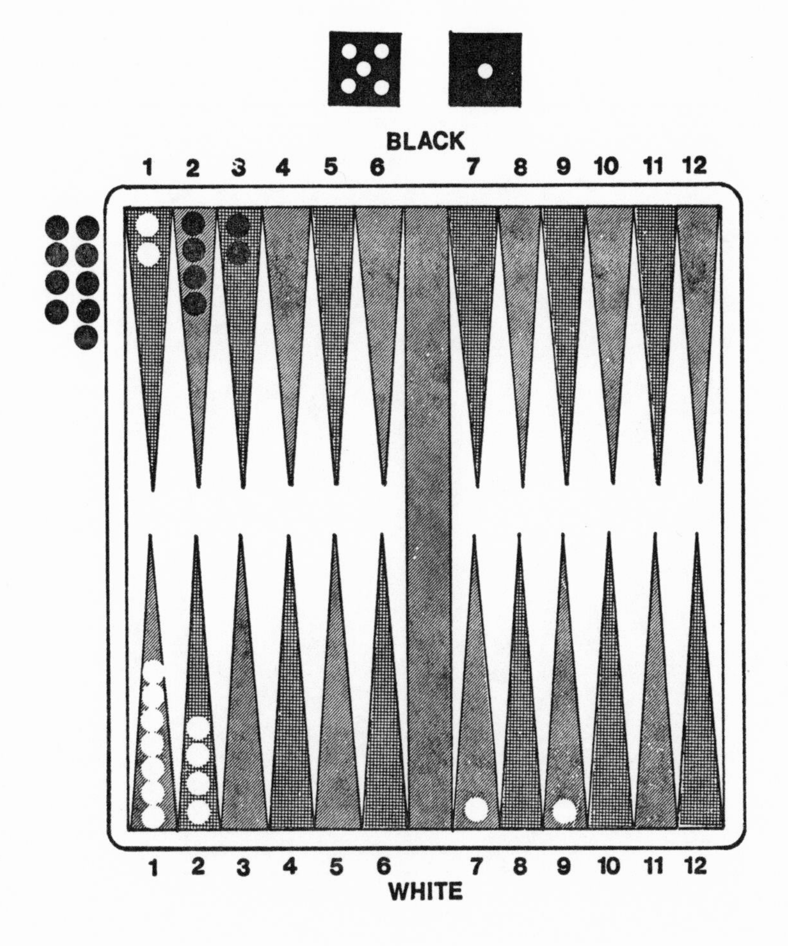

Black's roll: 5–1
(Diagram 23)

White moves from 9–W to 5–W and from 7–W to 5–W. The fact that White "makes" his 5-point is purely coincidental, as it has no purpose now. Since White is keeping both back men in readiness for another Black blot, these were the only moves he could make.

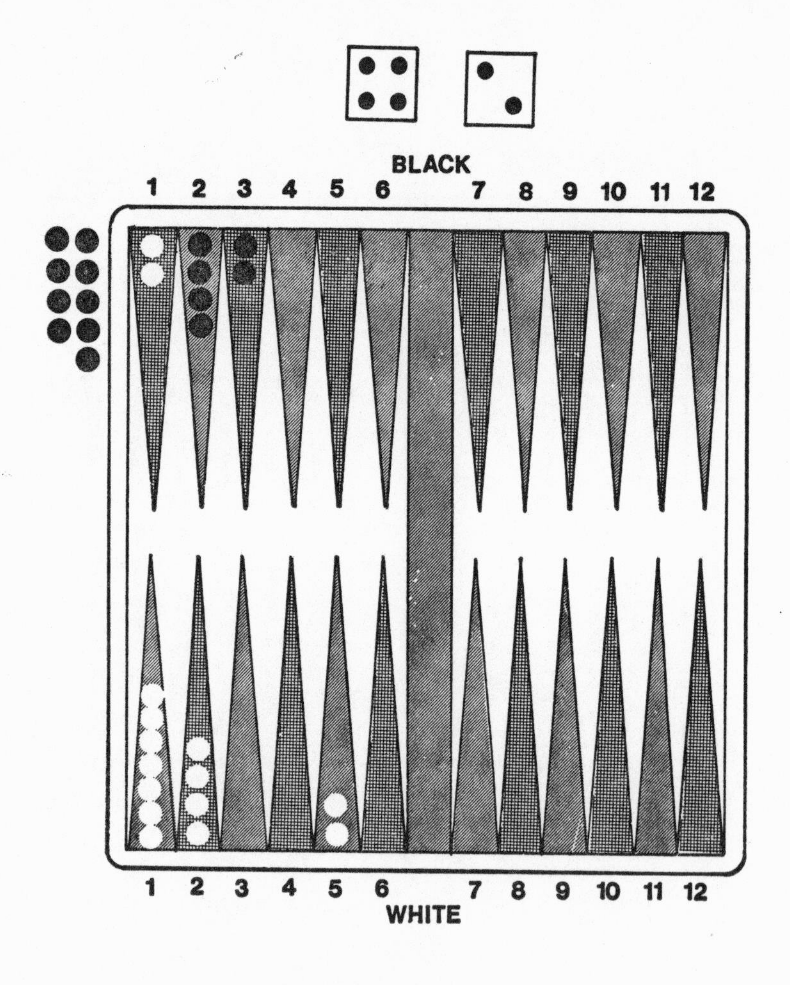

White's roll: 4–2
(Diagram 23–A)

Even this low roll enables Black to bear off two stones: one from 3–B, the other from 2–B. That leaves a blot on 3–B, but if White fails to hit it, Black will have a good chance of winning in two more rolls, which will give Black a backgammon or "triple game," unless White gets both his runners off Black's inner table by rolling a double higher than 2–2, or hits the Black blot.

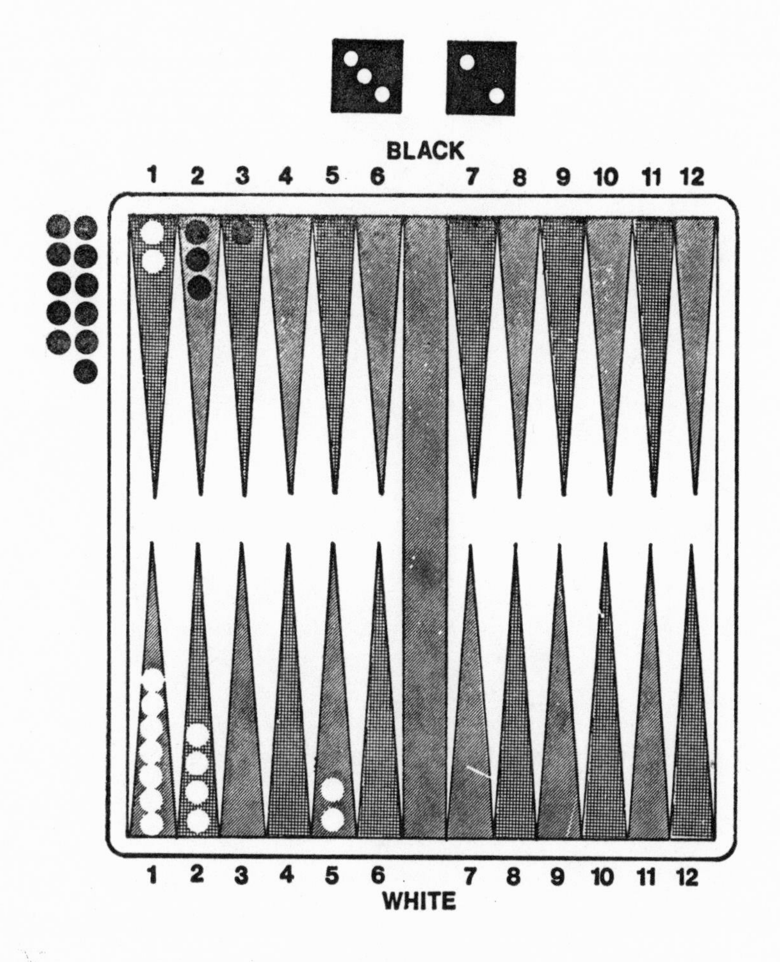

Black's roll: 3–2
(Diagram 24)

White moves from 1–B to 3–B, hitting a Black blot at last. From 3–B, White continues on to 7–B. White is hoping that this runner will hit the Black runner after Black reenters it, thus sending it to the bar again.

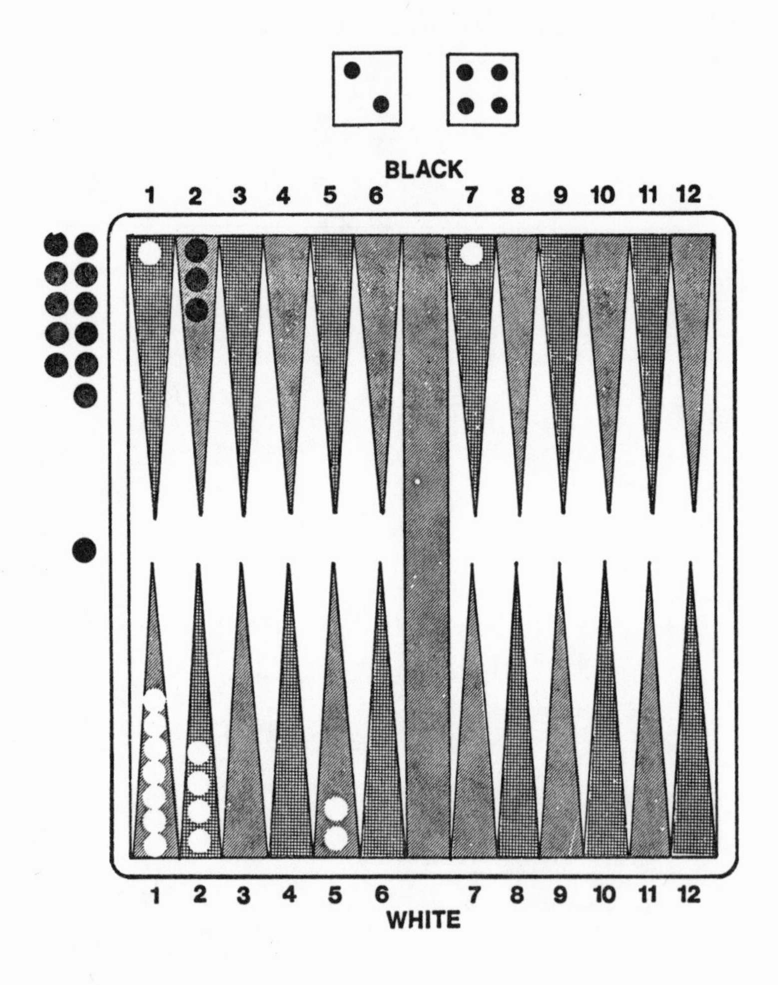

White's roll: 2–4
(Diagram 24–A)

Though 27 rolls out of a possible 36 would enable Black to reenter, Black fails to come up with one. Oddly, the fact that White made his 5–point proved the deciding factor, though it seemed quite trivial at the time. So Black stays on the bar.

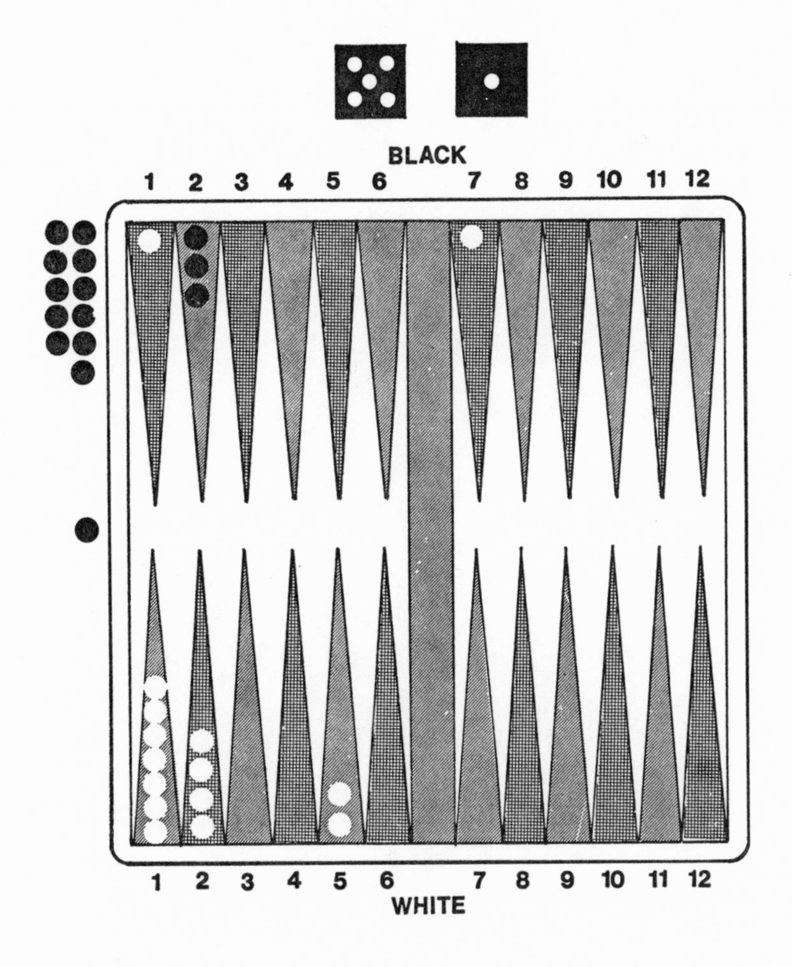

Black's roll: 5–1
(Diagram 25)

White moves his runner from 7–B to 12–B, He still has hopes of hitting a Black blot on a forthcoming roll and is keeping his back man in reserve for that purpose, in case his runner should miss.

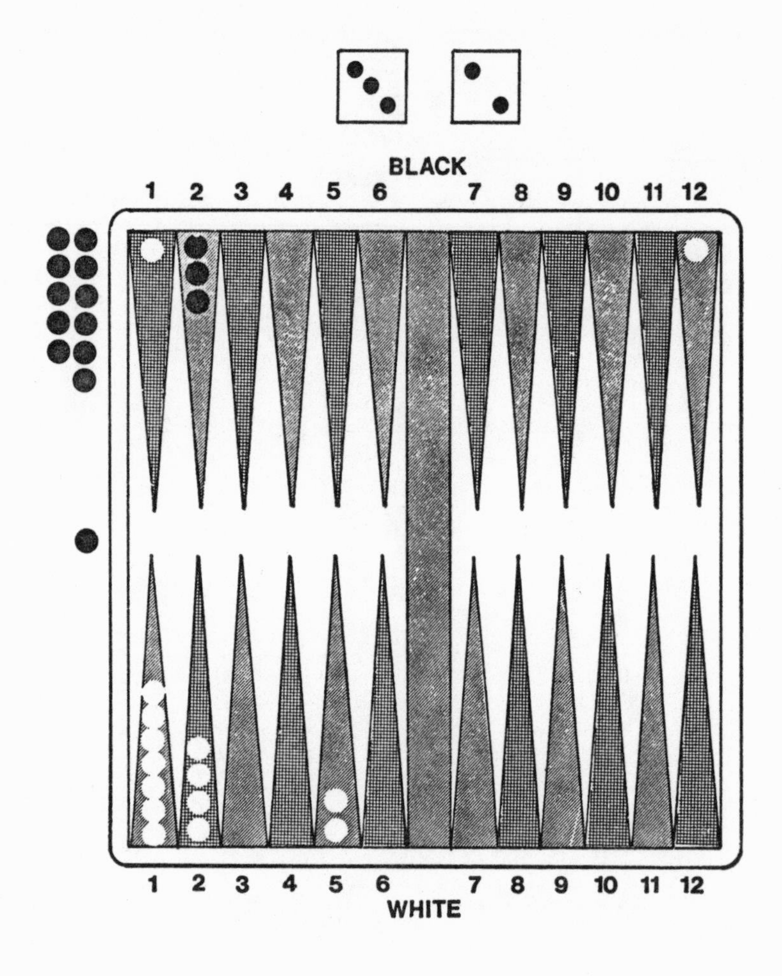

White's roll: 3–2
(Diagram 25–A)

Black reenters with his 4 and uses his 5 to advance from 4–W to 9–W, which is his only possible move. Here, the odds become significant. There are 15 chances out of a possible 36 that White's next roll will hit the Black blot. So the odds are seven to five in Black's favor.

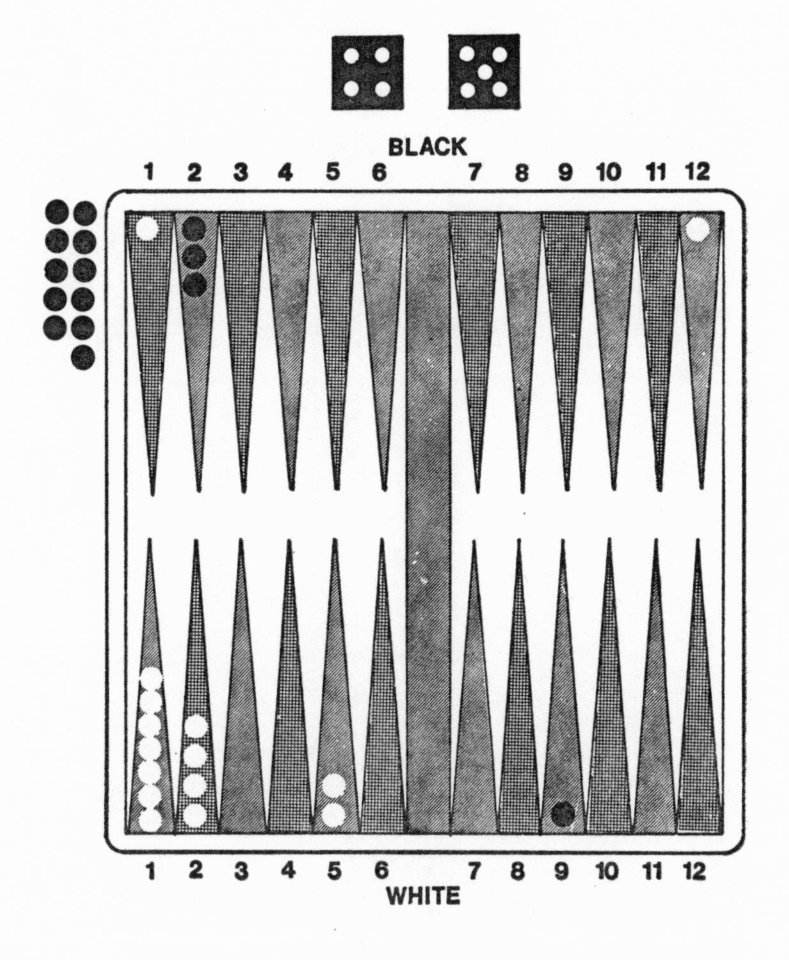

Black's roll: 4–5
(Diagram 26)

White moves from 12–B to 1–W, passing the Black blot on the way. Perhaps White should have stopped his runner at 7–W; then brought his back man from 1–B to 1–7. Either way would be making the best of a bad situation. By holding his back man on 1–B, White at least was able to postpone his decision.

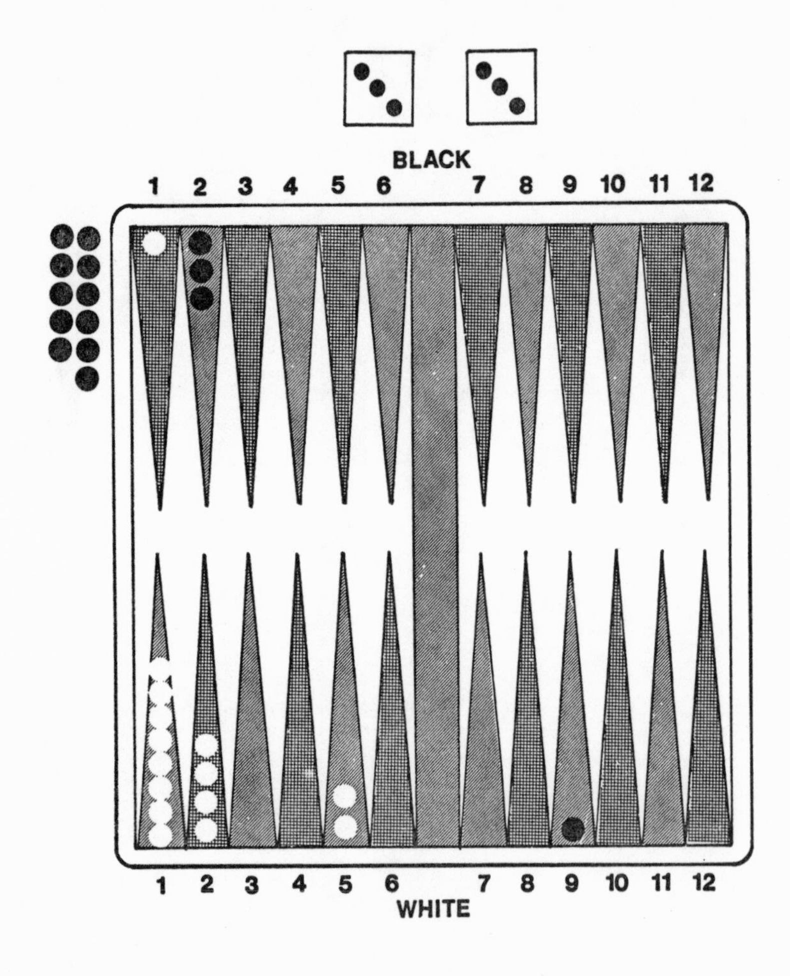

White's roll: 3–3
(Diagram 26 A)

Black uses this big roll to move from 9–W to 6–B, reaching his inner table, where he can again bear off. If he can do it in two rolls, he has a good chance of getting a gammon. Provided, of course, that White's last back man doesn't hit Black's last blot.

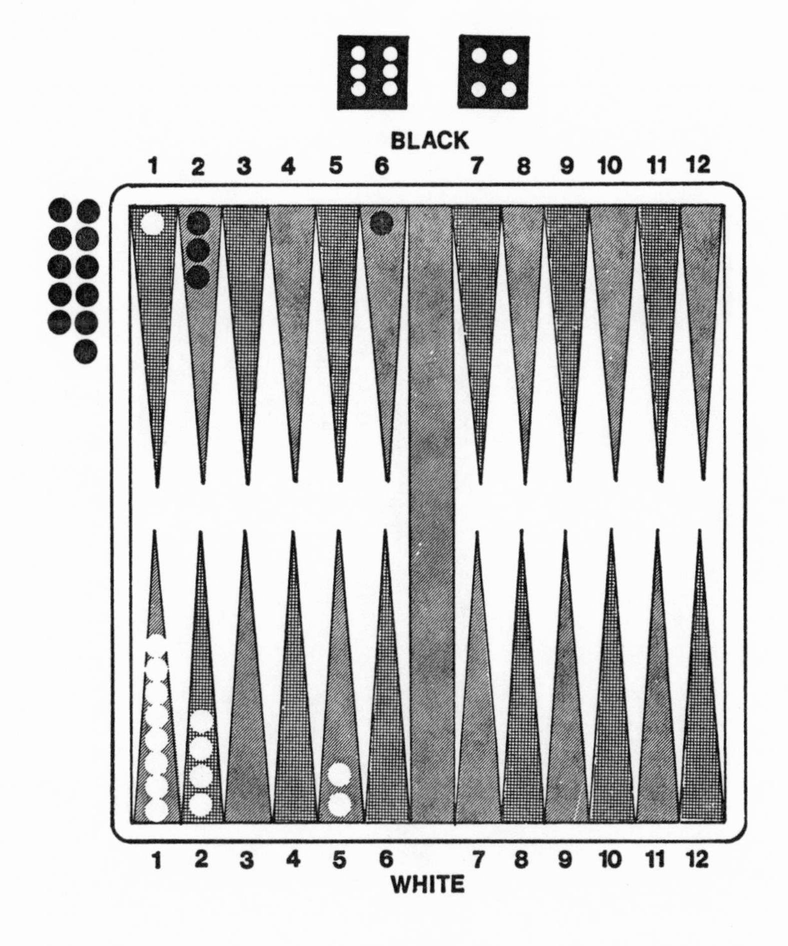

Black's roll: 6–4
(Diagram 27)

White does hit the black blot. He moves from 1–B to 6–B, scores his hit, and keeps on to 8–B. Black's chances of getting that gammon look bleak indeed, unless he rolls a couple of double 6s in succession.

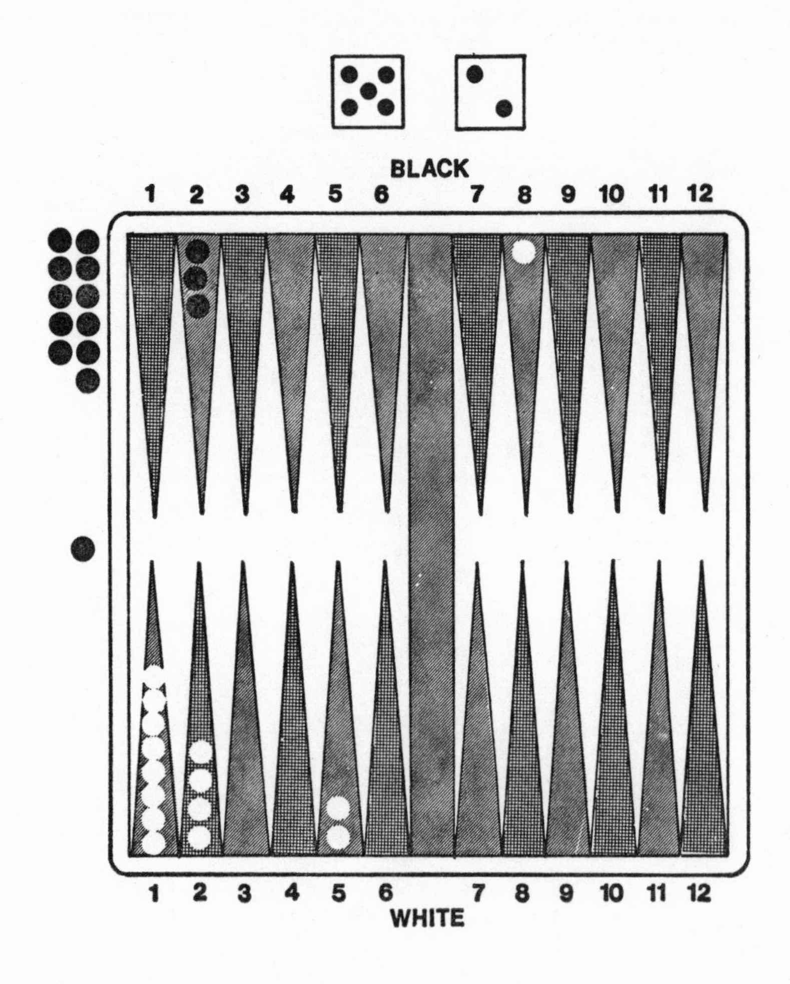

White's roll: 5–2
(Diagram 27–A)

By using the 4 and then the 5, Black enters on 4–W and moves to 9–W as his first step along the return trail which should give him an easy win, though his chances of scoring a gammon now look slim.

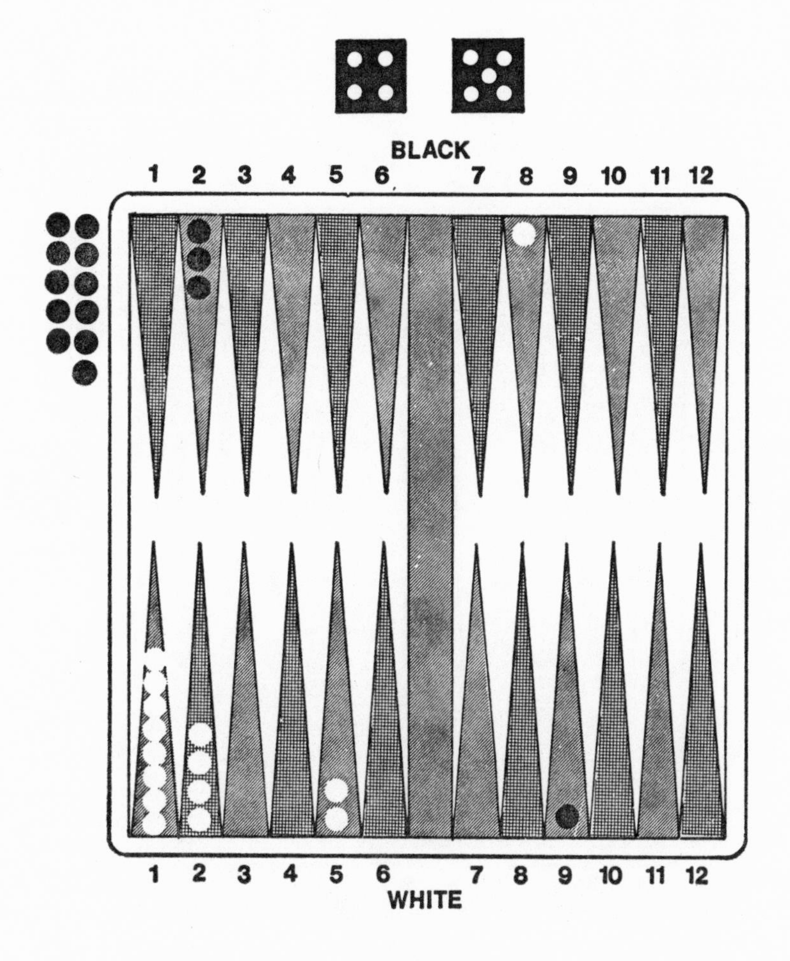

Black's roll: 4–5
(Diagram 28)

Again, a timely roll enables White to hit the Black blot by moving from 8–B to 9–W (2 + 2 + 2 + 2). One more roll can enable White to start bearing off his men, saving him from being gammoned. This shows how swiftly the scene can change in the final stages of a backgammon game.

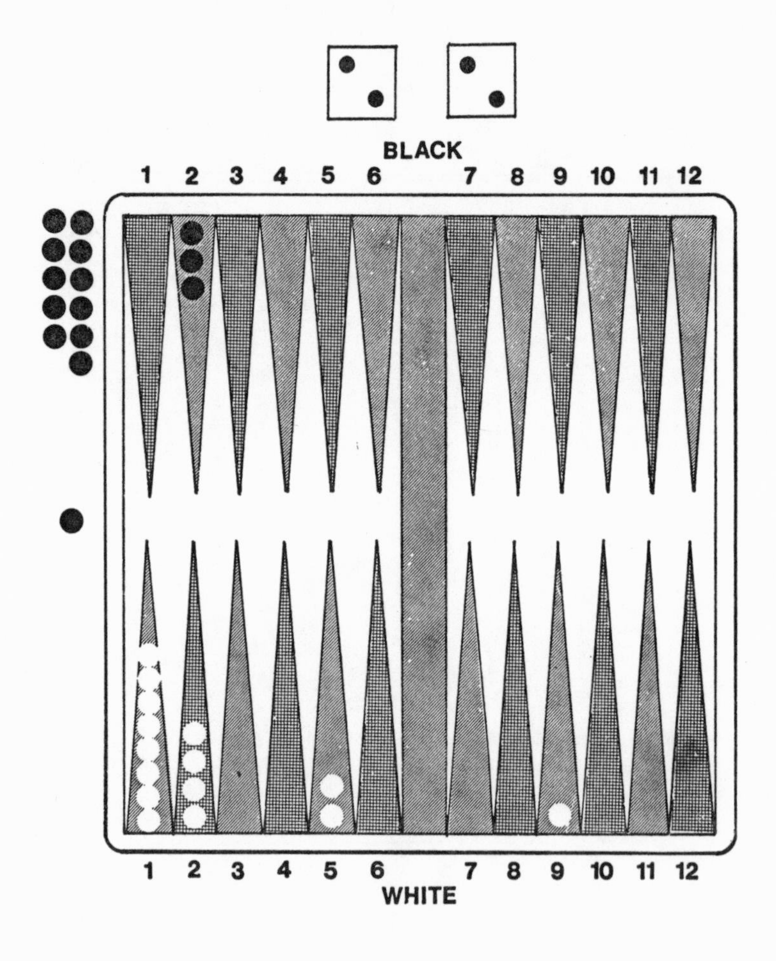

White's roll: 2–2
(Diagram 28–A)

Black enters on 6–W and moves to 9–W, hitting the White blot and sending it to the bar. Again, the tide has turned, and if Black can outroll White down the home stretch, he may score that gammon after all.

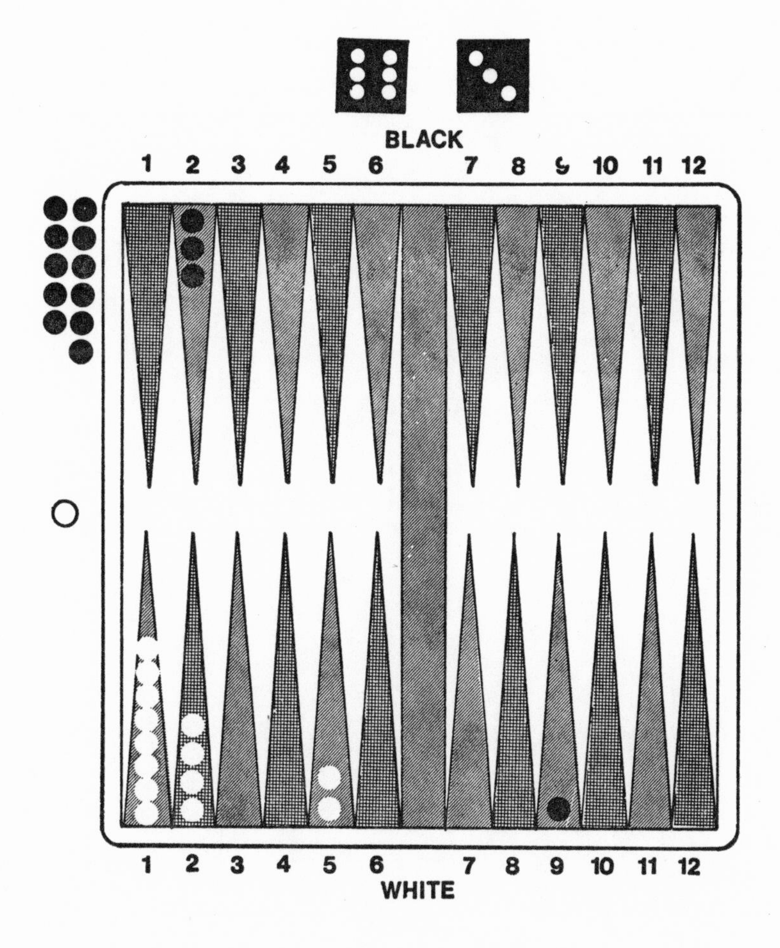

Black's roll: 6–3
(Diagram 29)

White enters on 5–B and moves to 9–B. Unless "blot meets blot," as they did before, this promises to be a photo finish, where the scoring of a gammon is concerned. Black is ahead by a move, but must bear off all his men before White bears off any.

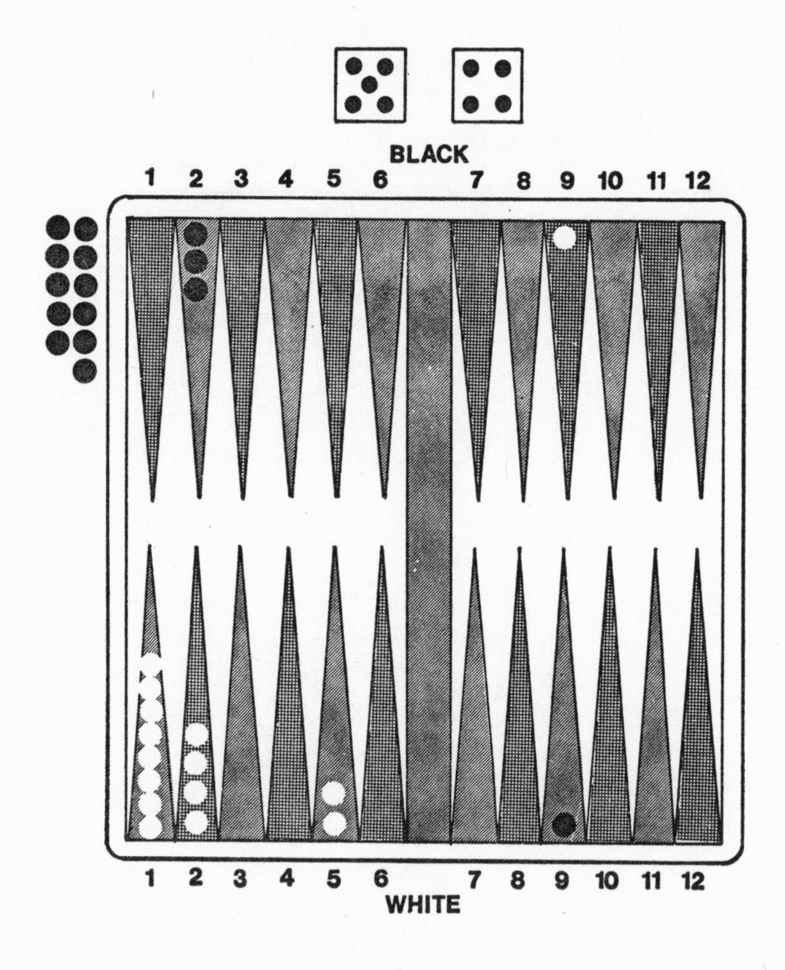

White's roll: 5–4
(Diagram 29–A)

Black wanted a roll that would bring his runner home and he got it. He moves from 9–W to 4–B (3 + 3 + 3 + 3). Note that this is as good as a 6–6, which would be limited to 6 + 6. A 5–5 would be better, bringing him clear to 1–B (5 + 5 + 5). But a 4–4 would have been best of all, bearing his stone off the board (4 + 4 + 4 + 4).

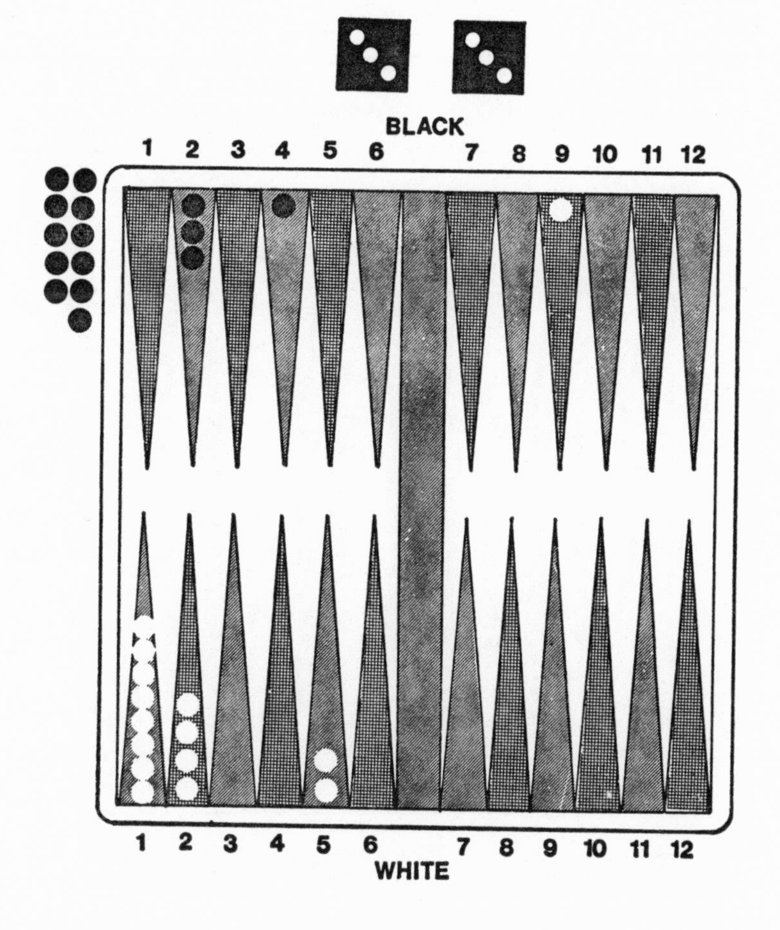

Black's Roll: 3–3
(Diagram 30)

White moves from 9–B to 10–W. White is worried because if Black rolls a 4–4, 5–5, or 6–6—one chance in twelve—Black will bear off all his men and White will be gammoned. The chance is small, but anything can happen at this stage of the game; and often, it does happen!

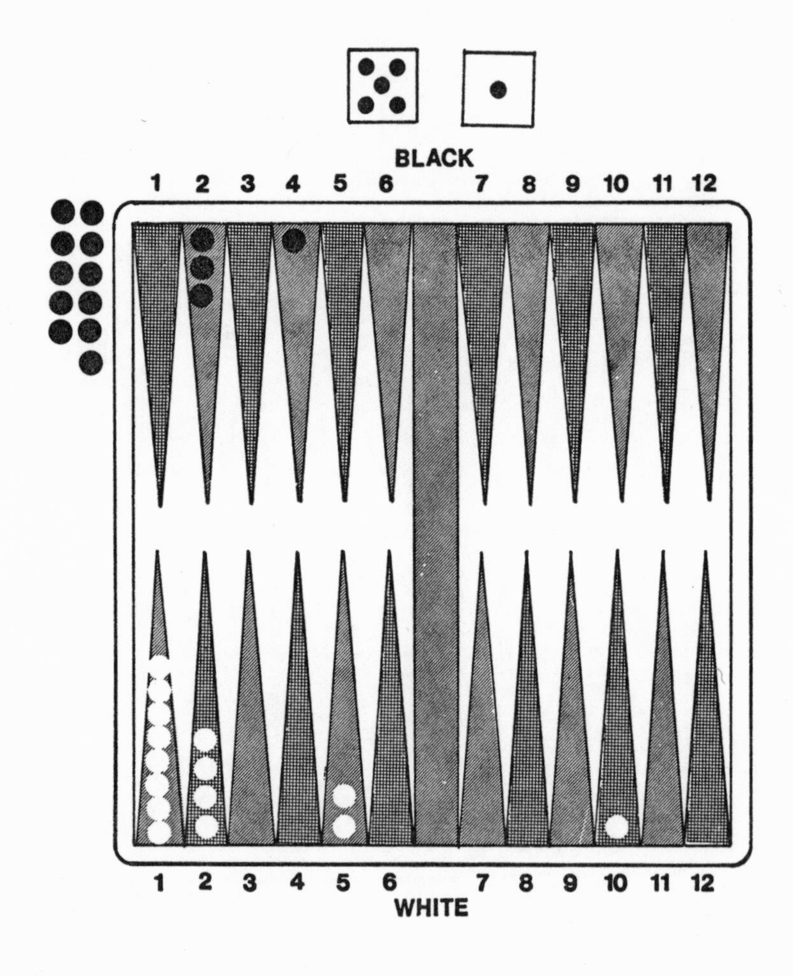

White's Roll: 5–1
(Diagram 30–A)

Black bears off from 4–B and also from 2–B. He thinks he has his gammon in the bag, because if White should also roll a 6–3, the best White could do would be to move from 10–W to 4–W with his 6; but he would then be unable to bear off with his 3. So Black sits very smug indeed.

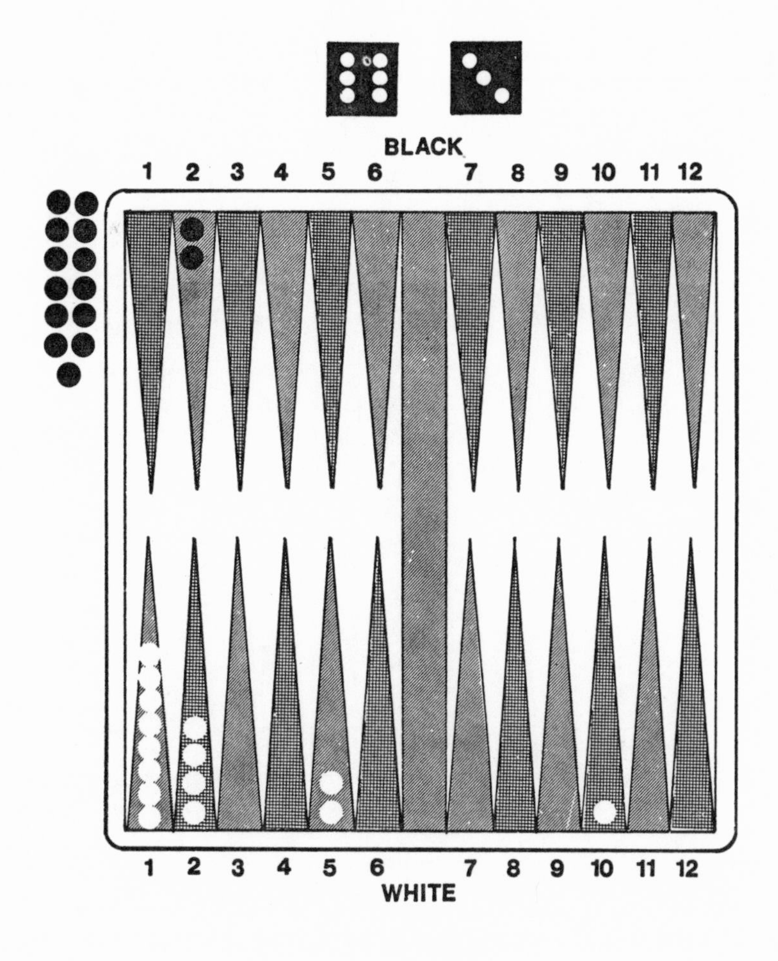

Black rolls 6–3
(Diagram 31)

This looks like a disappointment, but say not so. White moves from 10–W to 5–W on his 5 and then bears off from 2–W on his 2. Note that if he had rolled a 5–3 or a 5–4, he could not have borne off, and would have been gammoned. As it was, the lesser roll of 5–2 saved him from a double loss. That's why backgammon is a great game!

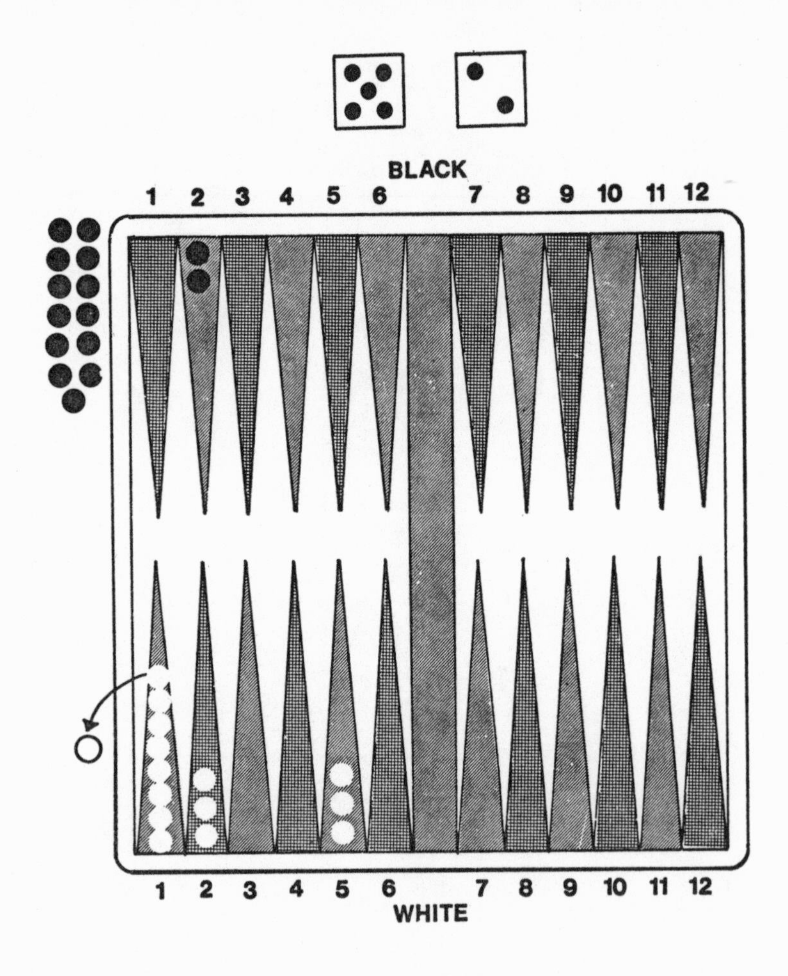

White rolls 5–2
(Diagram 31–A)

III

Starting the Game

IN TODAY'S BACKGAMMON, THE CUSTOMARY WAY TO begin the game is to have each player roll a single die with the understanding that whoever rolls the higher number, White or Black, makes the initial play, using the numbers showing on both dice. This gets the game underway automatically, unless each player happens to roll the same number. That means that they must roll again; and if further ties result, they must roll again—and still again—until one player hits a higher number than the other. That is the roll that stands.

The first roll is quite important as it gives the successful player a slight edge that may loom to formidable proportions near the end of the game. Often, no matter how the tides of battle may have zigzagged back and forth, the closing moments reach a situation where both players are bearing off stones at a similar pace with each threatening to triumph in the neck-to-neck finish. So it stands to reason that unless one falters, the player who had the first roll will go out ahead of his opponent, since he will have the benefit of an extra roll.

So if White gets the first roll, he does have an advantage, however slight; but Black, in his turn, may offset it, thanks to an advantage of his own. Out of thirty-six possible combinations that may turn up on a pair of dice, there are six that White will be unable to make on his first roll. Those are double 1, double 2, double 3, double 4, double 5 and double 6. With the exception of double 5, these rank among the best rolls that a player would want at the start of the game. So if Black rolls one, he may be quite glad that he did not get the first chance. Moreover, he may find himself practically a jump ahead of White, instead of things being the other way about.

Before analyzing the various opening rolls and suggesting how they should be played, it should be made clear that they apply in great degree to both players. What's good for White as the first roller can be just as good for Black, the second roller; and sometimes the opening procedure carries on from there. There are times, however, when this strikes an immediate snag, forcing a departure from standard practice. White, as first roller, *always* can move in accepted fashion. So can Black, the second roller, *unless* his roll comes in conflict with the move already made by White. In that case, Black must adjust his opening move accordingly, for reasons which are usually quite obvious.

To cover this amply, all of White's opening rolls will be listed in descending order (from 6–5 down to 2–1) with the moves that are usually recommended. It will be understood that these apply to Black's turn as well, but with certain exceptions that will be noted in brief. Following that, a listing will be given of the doubles (from 6–6 down to 1–1) which are exclusively Black's opening moves and generally can be handled in standard form, though here again, occasional exceptions may occur.

Table of White's Opening Moves
(Excluding doubles)

6–5: Affectionately known as "lover's leap," this enables White to take off from Black's ace-point, 1–B, and finish with a happy landing on 12–B, along with his own stones already stationed there. Since he advances his "runner" the maximum distance, with no danger, this can prove an excellent opening, if subsequent moves keep up a fast pace. Leaving a blot on 1–B means nothing, because if it is hit, White can reenter it with any roll except a 6, this early in the game.

For Black, this is an equally good opener, but it can not be used if White has placed two men on his own bar-point (7–W) as Black can not use 6–5 to move from 1–W to either 6–W or 7–W. About his only out is to move one man from 12–W to 7–B and another from 12–W to 8–B. This puts a blot on Black's own bar-point, but if White doesn't hit it, Black may be able to bring up a builder to join it, "making" his bar-point. A good gamble under the circumstances.

6–4: This is as bad as 6–5 is good. White moves from 1–B to 11–B, which is like taking a lover's leap but landing one step short, as it puts a White blot on B–11. However, it is a well-calculated risk, for if Black fails to hit the blot, White will have a good running start. White can play this roll safe by moving a stone from W–8 to W–2 and another from W–6 to W–2, thus making his own 2-point, but it is rather foolish to advance that far so soon, and good players decry the practice.

For Black, this is a fine first move if White has put a blot on 5–W, 7–W, or 11–W as Black can hit any one of those and send it to the bar in the course of his standard move (from 1–W to 11–W). It simply depends on whether Black uses his 4 first, his 6 first, or both together as 10. It is occasionally possible for Black to hit two White blots (one on 5–W, the other on 11–W) with this caper. (Also one on 6–W, the other on 11–W.)

6–3: Many players treat this as a lesser lover's leap, advancing a single runner from 1–B to 10–B, where it becomes a blot. Nothing wrong about that, but others prefer to move one stone from 1–B to 7–B and another from 12–B to 10–W. When they are so placed, Black can't hit both blots on the same roll.

For Black, the standard 6–3 move from 1–W to 10–W is fine if he can hit a White blot in the process. He could also switch to the alternative of 1–W to 7–W and 12–W to 10–B if it offers a hit. Other chances for a hit should also be considered.

5–4: The old reliable system was for White to move from 1–B to 10–B, exactly as with a 6–3 roll. That is still a good start for a running game, but many modern players prefer to move one stone from 1–B to 5–B for the 4 and 12–B to 8–W for the 5. If the White blot on 5–B is hit, it can be promptly reentered and in the meantime, White has the benefit of an additional stone on 8–W.

For Black, the old style opening is a natural response if White has placed a blot on 5–W or 10–W, as Black can knock off either. Other opportunities for hits can be considered. A good gimmick for Black is to move one stone from 12–W to 8–B and another from 12–W to 9–B.

6–2: Again, many players like to advance a runner as far as possible, in this case from 1–B to 9–B. If White's blot (on 9–B) should be hit by Black, White still might hit back, and if he does, Black will lose more points than White. An alternative is for White to move a single stone from 12–B to 5–W. If Black fails or hesitates to hit the White blot, White can move up a builder—as from 6–W, 8–W, or 12–B to 5–W—thus making his 5-point.

With Black, the situation is similar when he rolls a 6–2.

But if White opened by putting a blot on 11–B, Black would be smart to hit it with his 2 roll by a move from 12–W to 11–B, using his 6 to move from 1–W to 7–W. More often, White will put a blot on 7–B, practically inviting Black to hit it, so that White can reenter and hit back. Some players consider it good strategy for Black to accept the challenge and use the 6 of a 6–2 roll to move from 12–B to 7–B, hitting the White blot. That leaves Black with a blot on 7–B, but if he can add a builder before White hits back, he will make his bar-point (7–B), which is a real achievement.

5–3: The old standby is for White to move one stone from 8–W to 3–W and another from 6–W to 3–W, making his 3-point. It is safe, sure, and a good start toward a prime. It is hard to pick a sounder move than this.

For Black, the same rule applies, unless White opened by moving a runner from 1–B to 10–B. Then Black can use his 5–3 to move one stone from 12–W to the safety of 8–B and another from 12–W to 10–B, hitting the White blot there. This nullifies White's opener and gives Black a good start instead.

6–1: The ideal opener. White moves one stone from 12–B to 7–W and another from 8–W to 7–W, making his bar-point (7–W). This gives White a "half-prime" of three blocks in a row (8–W, 7–W, 6–W) and prevents Black from moving his runners (from 1–W) if he makes such big rolls as 6–6, 6–5, or 5–5.

For Black, the same procedure should be followed, consisting of moves from 12–W to 7–B and 8–B to 7–B. This is very gratifying if White opened by putting a blot on 7–B, where Black can knock it off while making his own bar-point.

5–2: A fairly safe and satisfactory play is for White to move one stone from 12–B to 8–W and another from 12–B to 11–W, where Black can only hit it by rolling 6–4 or 5–5, one chance in eleven. For absolute security, White could make a single move from 12–B to 6–W, but it is better to place the extra man on 8–W, so it is worth risking the blot on 11–W.

For Black, this is a good opener, too, and all the nicer if White happened to roll 6–5 to start, putting a blot on 11–B for Black to knock off, by moving one stone from 12–W to 11–B; the other from 12–W to 8–B.

4–3: By moving from 12–B to 9–W and from 12–B to 10–W, White puts two blots in jeopardy, but since Black can't hit both blots at once, the moves are worth the risk. If White does lose a blot, he will have a chance to hit back with another stone from 12–B. This is preferable to the "safety play" of moving one stone from 12–B to 6–W, for White's blots can prove valuable as builders.

For Black, the same play, in his case 12–W to 9–B and 12–W to 10–B, is particularly good if White has already put a blot on either of those points where Black can hit it. But if White opened by moving a runner from 1–B to 2–B, 5–B, or 7–B, the chances of a Black blot being hit are so greatly increased that Black can do better with a different form of response. By moving a stone from 12–W to 10–B and another from 1–W to 5–W, Black puts a builder (10–B) and a runner (5–W) both in action, so if either is knocked off, he can gear his game to suit the other.

5–1: White has to risk a blot on this opening roll, so it has long been considered good strategy to put it where it will do the most good if the gamble succeeds. White moves one stone from 12–B to 8–W and another from 6–W to 5–W. Unless Black hits the blot on 5–W, White will have good chances of bringing a builder from 6–W, 8–W, or even 12–B to make his 5-point, giving him a strong advantage.

For Black, this opener, 12–W to 8–B and 6–B to 5–B, is practically a must if White made an opening move that put a White blot on 5–B. In contrast, if White started with a move from 1–B to 2–B, Black will be taking too big a risk if he tries to make his own 5-point with a 5–1 roll. Alternatives are for Black to move one stone from 12–W to 8–B, another from 1–W to 2–W. Or he may do well with a single move from 1–W to 7–W (treating his roll as 1–5), getting his runner off to a fair start. That means putting a Black blot on 7–W, but if hit, it won't be very costly for Black.

4–2: The accepted opening for this roll is not only good, but obvious. White moves one stone from 8–W to 4–W; another from 6–W to 4–W, making hiw 4-point (4–W) just that easily.

For Black, in his turn, the same moves are every bit as good. Coming from 8–B to 4–B and from 6–B to 4–B, he makes his 4-point in the accepted manner. If White happened to put a runner on 11–W, 9–W, or 7–B, Black might be tempted to move from 12–W and hit the White blot, but it might be wiser for Black to resist that urge.

4–1: In the Victorian Era, White was apt to play this opener safe by moving a single stone from 12–B to 8–W, which would give him an extra stone on his 8-point, but that became outmoded. The preferred plan is to move a stone from 12–B to 9–W and another from 1–B to 2–B. This leaves three White blots but one on 9–W is not risky and if Black is foolish enough to hit a White blot on 1–B or 2–B, White can immediately reenter it, with a chance of hitting Black's blot in the process.

With Black, a copy of the modern opening move is good, unless White has split his runners by moving one from 1–B to 2–B or from 1–B to 3–B. In that case, White will have two chances of hitting Black's blot on 9–B with different throws of the dice. Also, if White has advanced both his runners to 3–B, 4–B, or to 7–B, the Black blot on 9–B can be hit with the roll of a single die, if Black uses the standard opening of 12–W to 9–B and 1–W to 2–W.

In any of those instances, Black can revert to the Victorian safety play, by simply moving one stone from 12–W to 8–B, giving him four blockers on each of those points, which represents a nicely balanced setup.

3–2: Again, White could open with the Victorian safety play of a single move from 12–B to 8–W, but the preferred opening is to put a White blot on 10–W and another on 11–W, by moving each from 12–B. The odds are against Black hitting either blot and he can't hit both on his first roll. If Black hits neither, White will have two builders on their way toward making a point, so this opening is well worth the risk.

With Black, the same first move is a logical response, unless White opened by splitting his runners. Then, it may be unwise for Black to risk two blots by moving one from 12–W to 11–B and another from 12–W to 10–B, as White would have better chance of hitting one. Instead, he could fall back on the safety play, by making a single move from 12–W to 10–B, as White would have a better chance of hitting one. Instead, he could fall back on the safety play, by making a single move from 12–W to 8–B, or follow any other course that expediency suggests.

3–1: As a fine opening roll, this ranks with 6–1. There, White made his own bar-point (7–W), while here he makes his own 5-point by moving one stone from 8–W to 5–W and another from 6–W to 5–W. This gives White an advantage that may prove of increasing value as the game proceeds.

With Black, a first roll of 3–1 should be treated in the same way, by moving from 8–B to 5–B and from 6–B to 5–B, making Black's 5-point. There is an added prospect, however, that can work to Black's immediate advantage. If White opened by moving a runner from 1–B to 5–B, Black will hit when making his 5-point. If White should follow with a big roll of 6–6, 6–5, or 5–5, he would be unable to reenter and would waste his roll.

2–1: With this feeble roll, White's simplest play is a single move from 12–B to 10–W, leaving a blot that Black can hit only with a 6–3 or 5–4. A more subtle procedure is for White to move one stone from 12–B to 11–W and another from 1–B to 2–B. Black has less chance of hitting White's blot on 11–W and will avoid hitting the one on 2–B for fear that White will reenter and hit back.

With Black, much depends on White's opening move. If White put a blot on 10–B, Black can knock it off with the simple 2–1 play of moving from 12–W to 10–B. If White put a blot on 11–B, Black can knock if off with the subtle process of moving from 12–W to 11–B and from 1–W to 2–W. If White did not advance either runner from 1–B, Black can resort to a risky opening, by bringing one stone from 12–W to 11–B and moving another from 6–B to 5–B. If either Black blot is hit, Black may find it handy as a "back man," while if he gets by with this caper, both blots can become promising builders.

Summary of White's Opening Moves

It must be remembered that the openings just listed are not adamant, but consist entirely of suggested procedures which experienced players have found most practical, just as with openings in chess, checkers, and various other board games. Nor are the potential openings limited to those listed. Over the years, many innovations have been introduced, some suited to certain types of play, others devised to meet exigencies in the course of a game.

In analyzing the fifteen opening rolls alreadly listed, four were quite as good for Black, the second roller, as for White, the first roller. Those four were 6–1, 5–3, 4–2, and 3–1, because in each case, a player using the recommended rolls will *make a point,* thus maintaining a position that is *free from blots.* This applies when Black rolls any of the doubles that follow, because in each case the recommended moves result in his *making a point, or points,* with *no blots.* However, in some cases White's preceding roll may block Black's intended moves, forcing Black to use a less desirable alternative. Such cases will be shown as they occur.

Table of Black's Opening Moves
(Consisting of doubles following White's opener)

Double 6: The biggest and often the best of Black's openers. He moves two stones from 1–W to 7–W, making his opponent's bar-point; and another pair from 12–W to 7–B, making his own bar point, thus attaining two important objectives in one timely swoop. But it is possible for White to foil this grand opening before it takes place, by rolling 6–1 on his first play and making his bar-point for himself.

In that case, Black simply can't move his two back men from 1–W to 7–W, because White has it made. Even worse, he can't move his back men at all, but he has to use those two 6's if he can. That leaves him two rather unhappy choices. He can move four stones from 12–W to 7–B, leaving a blot on 12–W; or he can move two from 12–W to 7–B, and two from 8–B to 2–B, making both his bar-point (7–B) and his 2-point (2–B), but leaving a blot on 8–B.

Don't shed a tear for Black. Either way, he has moved his maximum of 24 points and has splendid chances of establishing a prime. In fact, a player who favors the "running game" in which the big objective is to "get there firstest with the mostest" may welcome this very situation.

Double 5: This is the maverick of doubles. There is only one thing that Black can really do with it. That is to move two stones from 12–W all the way to 3–B. But is that so bad? If a few nice rolls follow, Black may be able to make a few more points on his inner table and find himself sitting pretty. Much prettier than if he had opened with a lot of lesser rolls that might have put him into trouble and nothing else.

One thing nice about this roll: mediocre though it may be, there is no way that White could have stopped it beforehand, as he could have flagged a Black double 6 with a 6–1 of his own. The more that Black looks at a double 5 opener and grieves over it, the more contented he should be that he didn't roll something worse; and that means a lot worse.

Double 4: Almost any moves are good with an opening roll of double 4, but the best balance is provided by having Black bring out two runners from 1–W to 5–W and two blockers from 12–W to 9–B, thus making White's 5-point and his own 9-point. But this desirable result will be stymied if White opened with the standard 3–1 move of making his own 5-point by putting two Whites on 5–W.

Black's best course, in that case, is to go tit-for-tat by making his own 5-point with a move of two stones from 12–W to 5–B. This gives him two extra stones on his own table, with prospects of rapidly establishing a prime. If White happened to put a blot on 5–B with his opening roll (such as 4–5 or 4–3), Black will automatically knock it off when making his 5-point. That brings up a still more pleasing prospect for Black, where a double 4 roll is concerned:

If White opened with a 4–3 or a 4–1, putting a blot on 9–W, Black's logical play of a double 4 opener would be to bring both runners from 1–W all the way to 9–W, establishing a block there and knocking off White's blot in the process. This gives Black a total of 16 points toward a running game, with his runners safe from attack; and he sets back White 16 points by sending his blot to the bar.

Double 3: The old reliable is for Black to bring his runners from 1–W to 4–W and another pair from 8–B to 5–B, making his 5-point. But this won't work if White already made his 4-point by putting two blockers on 4–W, as he could with a 4–2 roll. Black's usual play in that case is to make his own 3-point and 5-point by carrying one pair of stones from 6–B to 3–B and another pair from 8–B to 5–B, with a few chances of hitting a White blot that might be on 5–B.

That, however, means that Black must leave a blot on his 8-point (8–B), so a safer and sometimes better course is for Black to make his own bar-point by bringing a pair from 12–W to 10–B and then on to 7–B. Safer, because it leaves no Black blot and definitely better whenever White opens by placing a blot on either 7–B or 10–B, which he is apt to do occasionally.

2–2: A sound opening is for Black to move his runners from 1–W to 3–W and on to 5–W, thus making White's 5–point, which is the point that White is most anxious to make. A fine start if White opened by putting a blot on his 5–point in hope of building there, as Black not only kills White's chance, but sends the White blot to the bar, giving it a long, long way to get back where it was. However, if White opened by making either his 5–point or his 3–point (5–W or 3–W) Black can't make this strong defensive move.

Few players worry about that. If Black is their color, they usually prefer the best alternative, which is to open by bringing two stones from 12–W to 11–B and another pair from 6–B to 4–B. That way, Black plants two blockers on 11–B with the prospect of turning them into builders and also makes his 4–point (4–B) which is a very good point to make.

1–1: Though this is the smallest possible roll of the dice, true backgammon enthusiasts regard it as the best opening throw that they could make. The reason is as simple as rolling off a log—or two logs. Black simply dumps a pair of stones from 8–B to 7–B, thus making his bar-point; and another pair from 6–B to 5–B, making his 5–point. With practically no effort, he has made the two most coveted points in the book and the fact that he left a blot on his 8–point (8–B) is too trivial to matter. This is truly Black's perfect opening move, because there is no way that White can prevent it. In contrast, this super-move can often give Black a bonus, by hitting a White blot on 5–B or 7–B, which White placed there with his opening move.

Or, more accurately, which White *misplaced* there. However you consider it, 1–1 is a very nice opening roll.

Summary of Black's Opening Moves

When Black rolls a double for his first move, it often enables him to decide upon the style of game that he should play; or looking at it the other way about, the roll may decide it for him. Taking the two best rolls, double 6 and double 1, as the extreme examples, it is quite obvious that 6–6 gives Black remarkable headway in outracing White and therefore should commit Black to what is termed a "running game"; while 1–1 enables Black to put so firm a clamp on White's inner table that Black has practically started a so-called "blocking game."

This applies in varying degree to other double rolls, though with those, Black has more of a choice. A player can hardly be fully committed to any form of play this early in the game, because a series of adverse rolls—his own or those of his opponent—can cause him to reappraise his prospects. Let's say White opens with a 6–5 and moves a runner from 1–B to the safety of 12–B. Black tops that with a double 6, making his own bar-point (7–B) and White's bar-point (7–W) as well. That would put Black ahead in a running game, but if White should roll a double 5 and make his own 3-point (by a double move from 12–B to 3–W), he would not only be right back in the running, but would be nicely ahead, if Black's next roll proved to be a feeble 2–1.

Admittedly, this would be an unusual case, but there are many times when White lands a double on his second roll and is able to make a standard move or a suitable alternative. This is particularly true when Black failed to make a double on his first roll. Similarly, if White fails to double on his second roll, Black stands a good chance of making a well-accepted move if he comes up with a double on *his* second roll.

Beyond that, things are apt to get fuzzier where doubles are concerned, but good players are often apt to improvise satisfactory moves with doubles, just as they do with ordinary rolls. It's all a part of the great game of backgammon, as more and more enthusiasts are finding out.

Options with Opening Moves

Until about the year 1900, the player gaining the opening move in backgammon was given two privileges: one, to move the number of spots on both dice, his own and his adversary's as already described; the other was to reject that total and roll the dice again, this time rolling both dice himself and taking the new total for his first play.

Unless the first total was highly desirable, such as 6–1, 3–1, or another good combination, the player usually would prefer to roll again, largely in the hope of rolling a double, which was impossible on the first roll, because the rule specified that if each player came up with the same number on his die, they would have to roll again.

By way of a simple example:

White rolls 3 and Black rolls 3. Both roll again.

White rolls 5 and Black rolls 4. White gets 5–4 for his first play, *if he wants.* Otherwise White rolls again, on his own, and comes up with 4–3, which he *must* use for his first roll.

Actually, this old-time rule still may stand. Backgammon is not only a time-honored pastime but a world-wide game as well. So anybody, anywhere, is privileged to dig up a century-old rulebook and go by what it says. However, it must be conceded that the first player gains an undue advantage if allowed to reject the first roll and begin all over.

To remedy that situation, a new rule was introduced during the early 1900s, to the effect that:

The players must each cast a single die for the privilege of first move, the higher winning. Ties throw again. By mutual consent, it may be agreed to let the higher throw play the points on his own and his adversary's die for the first move; otherwise, he must throw again with two dice.

This handles the situation very nicely. The players each rolled a single die to see who had the first move. As soon as that was settled, the high man made a regular roll, giving him a chance to start the game with a double, if he was lucky enough to get one. They could go back to the old rule of using the numbers on each single die, but if they agreed upon that, it meant that the roll would have to stand.

This modified rule was well accepted in America when backgammon had a wave of popularity during the 1930s. At that time, various clubs decided to adopt a standard code of rules to be used in tournament play. They went along with the idea of letting each player roll a single die, with the high determining who was to play first and the total of the dice representing the amount of his roll, which must stand exactly as it is.

Because this is the most recent form of opening procedure and the one most frequently cited in modern descriptions of backgammon, it therefore has been given precedence in this book as well. As a result, the discussions of opening moves throughout this chapter have been on that basis. However, that does not rule out the older procedures, particularly in strictly social play. While you are reading this, thousands of backgammon enthusiasts in many lands and climes may right now be rattling the dice for a second opening roll and hoping for a double, blithely unaware that it has been ruled out in some highly select but extremely limited circles.

The one essential difference to be considered is this: If White, as opener, is given the privilege of a second roll, he will have one chance in six of rolling a double. If he does, that double will be entirely untrammeled, because all stones—White and Black—will be in the original setup. White, therefore, can follow the preferred recommendations for double 6 or double 3, as well as others. In short, the "Table of Black's Opening Moves" will apply to White instead, but with no restrictions.

As for Black, the table will still apply to his opening moves, exactly as they have been described, unless White was lucky enough to open with a double, thanks to his extra roll. In that case, Black may find himself somewhat stymied if he should roll a double of his own. This means that when White has the opening roll with doubles allowed, Black's first roll becomes the equivalent of White's second roll, as described earlier, and should be so treated.

IV

Forward and Backward Methods

BACKGAMMONITES OF THE VICTORIAN ERA DIVIDED THE play into two distinct categories as it progressed: The "forward game" and the "backward game." Those terms still are applicable in a general way, so it is worth while considering them as such. To a degree, they are automatic, since they depend on whether a player gets high rolls or low rolls with the dice. High rolls naturally encourage the forward game, because they enable a player to move stones fast from his opponent's table into his own inner table. Low rolls retard a player's progress, forcing him to adopt a backward game.

The difference between the techniques of these two games can be put very simply. In the forward game, since the player is ahead or hopes to get ahead, he should use his rolls to go ahead as rapidly as possible, avoiding certain risks. In the backward game, since the player is behind, he should stay behind as long as possible, hoping to delay his adversary in order to catch up and even taking risks that may help to achieve that aim.

Now it is quite obvious that at certain times both players will be playing a forward game if their rolls are consistently above average. Conversely, they will both tend toward a backward game if their rolls are below par. At times, they will be in opposition, forward versus backward; but more often they will be fluctuating from one form of game to the other, not really knowing which course they should decide upon. As a result, a player may often find it expedient to follow an in-between course that will allow him to shift either way, as required. Because of that, modern backgammon players speak in terms of three categories: the "running game," the "blocking game," and the "back game."

Of these, the running game is definitely an extension of the old forward game, in which the player decides to outrace his adversary. The blocking game may be used by a player to keep himself in the running, or to recover from a few low rolls; hence, in a sense, it represents a compromise between a forward and a backward game and may veer toward one or the other. The back game is distinctly a backward game which has reached the stage where a player must utilize drastic measures in order to ward off defeat.

These factors will be easily recognized by studying a few examples of each type, as follows:

The Running Game

Suppose that White gains the opening move with a 6–5, and naturally moves a back man from 1–B to 12–B, which is practically a commitment to a forward game; and why not? White's next roll may be a fizzle, but he's already that far ahead. So it is up to Black to show his mettle. So Black does, with what many connoisseurs of backgammon regard as the ideal roll, a 4–4.

They regard it as the "ideal" because they say that there is no wrong way to play it. Some critics disagree with this, on the ground that anyone following a fleeting whim may be passing up something better. One such whim is to jump the gun and make a run for it with a move of two stones from the opposing 1–point to the opposing 9–point. That would mean a double move by Black from 1–W to 9–W, which in this case is quite justified.

Since White used his roll of 11 to dispatch a runner to the safety of the "comfort station" at 12–B, Black uses his bigger roll of 16 to advance both his runners from 1–B to a secure position at 9–B. That leaves the board in the situation shown in Diagram R–1.

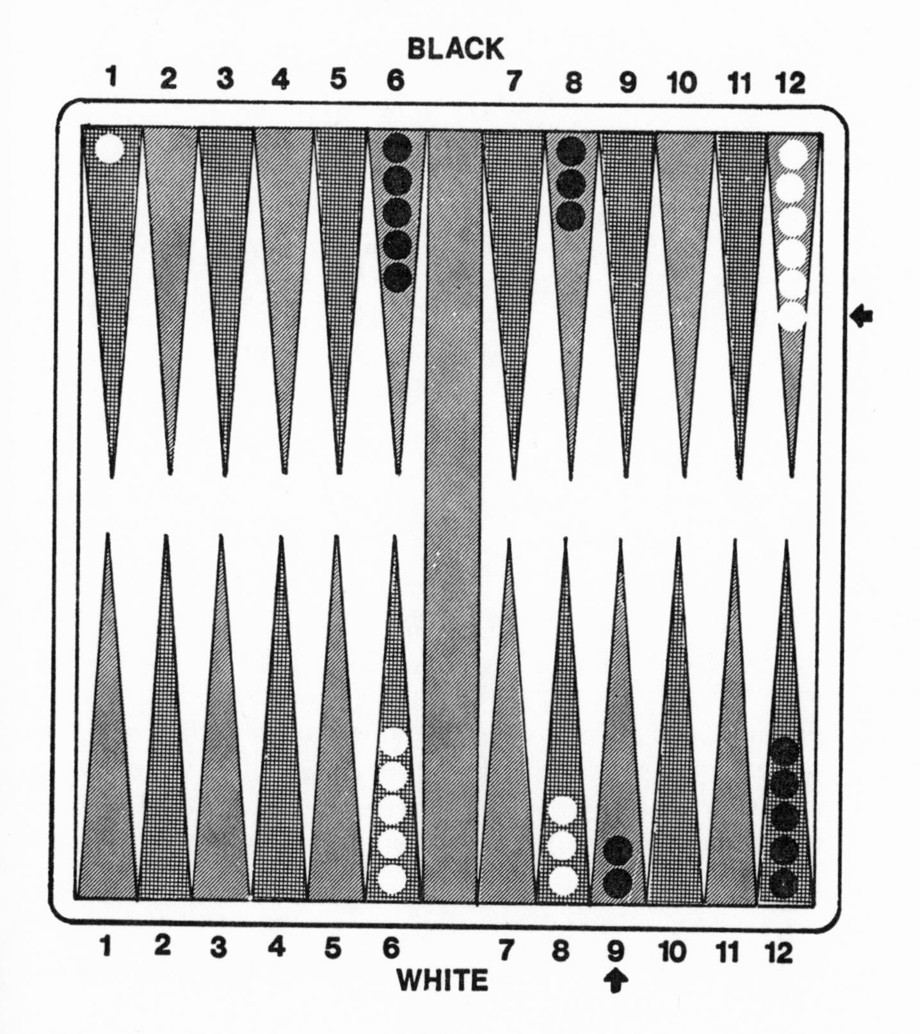

R–1

Naturally, White is irked by Black's bit of luck, so when White rolls a 5–4, he uses it to bring his second runner from 1–B to 10–B. He has to move the 4 first (1–B to 5–B) and then the 5 (5–B to 10–B) which does the trick very neatly. That puts a White blot on 10–B, but if Black manages to hit it at this juncture, White doesn't care, as the chances are that White can hit back.

However, Black doesn't have a chance to hit the White blot. Black gets a meager roll of 1–1, which is a disappointment. As an opener, Black could have used it to make his bar-point (7–W) and his 5-point (5–W) in the commonly accepted style. But now, those two points don't matter, for White has brought both his runners past them. Black can't move from 12–W to 12–B, so he simply pushes up his two runners from 9–W to 11–W, getting them that much farther on their way. That leaves the board as shown in Diagram R–2.

Any roll totaling 5 or more (with the exception of 3–3) would enable White to go past the intervening Blacks on 12–W and 11–W. But all White manages to get is a 2–1. That, however, does not discommode him. He moves his blot from 10–B to the security of 12–B and another stone from 8–W to 7–W. Black, too, fails to get by as hoped, but his roll of 6–1 enables him to spread his runners safely, moving one from 11–W to 8–B and dropping off the other at the "comfort station" on 12–W. That puts the board as shown in Diagram R–3.

For all practical purposes, this has already become a full-fledged running game in which each player is about to outrace the other to the finish. White must take the precaution of moving a single stone from 12–B; then moving the remaining six in pairs or not at all, so as not to leave a blot on 12–B. By the same token, Black must make all his moves in pairs from 12–W so as not to leave a blot there.

As it happens, White rolls 3–2 and moves a pair to start

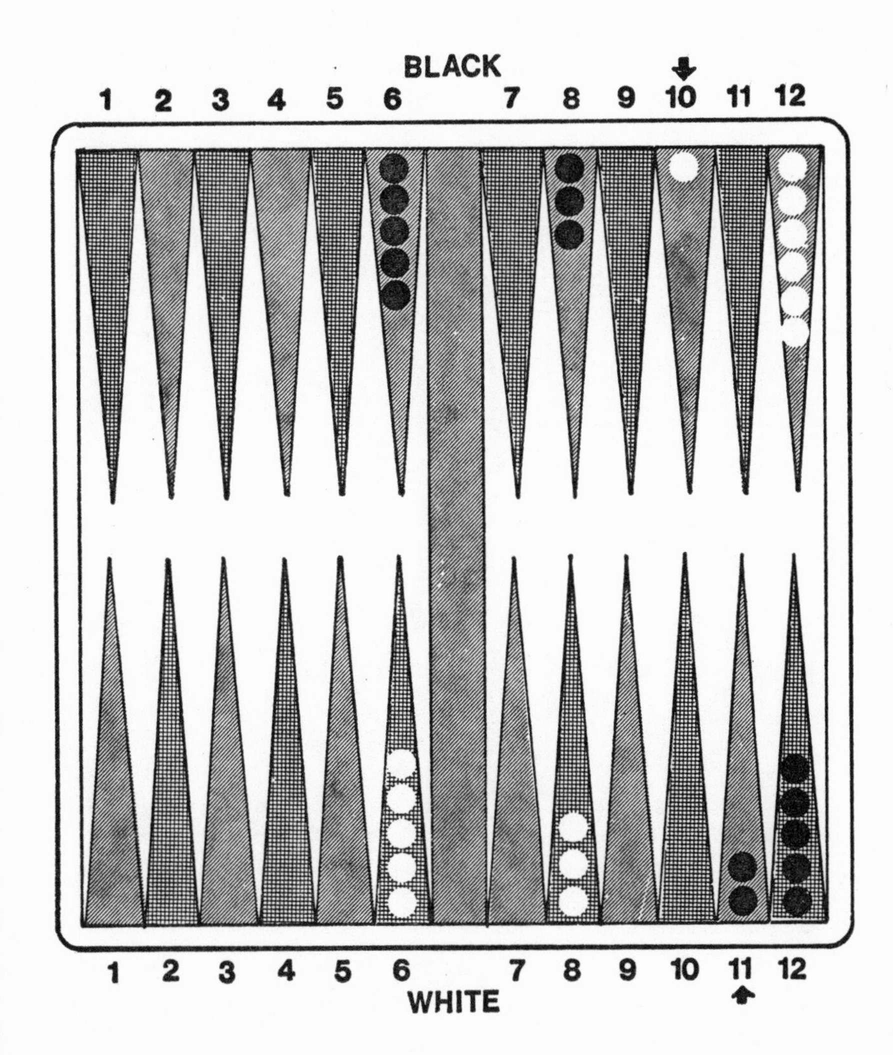

R–2

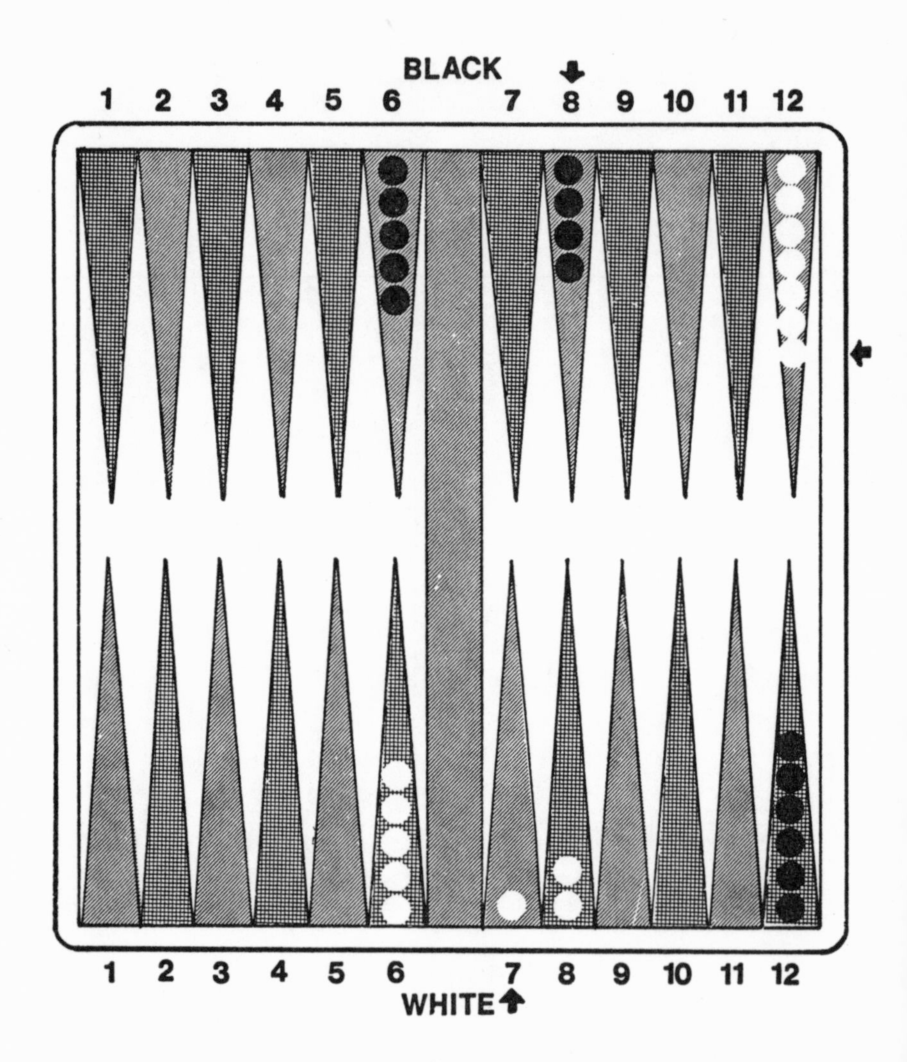

R–3

from 12–B to 10–W and 11–W, getting past 12–W, which is so heavily held by Black. (White is reserving his move of a single stone from 12–B until later.) Black rolls 2–2 and moves *two pairs* (four in all) from 12–W to 11–B. That leaves the board as shown in Diagram R–4.

White proceeds to roll 5–1, which is made to his order, as he wants to move a single stone from 12–B, so that he will leave an even number there. So he uses his 5–1 to move a lone stone from 12–B to 8–W and on to 7–W. Black rolls a 3–2 and simply moves two stones from 12–W

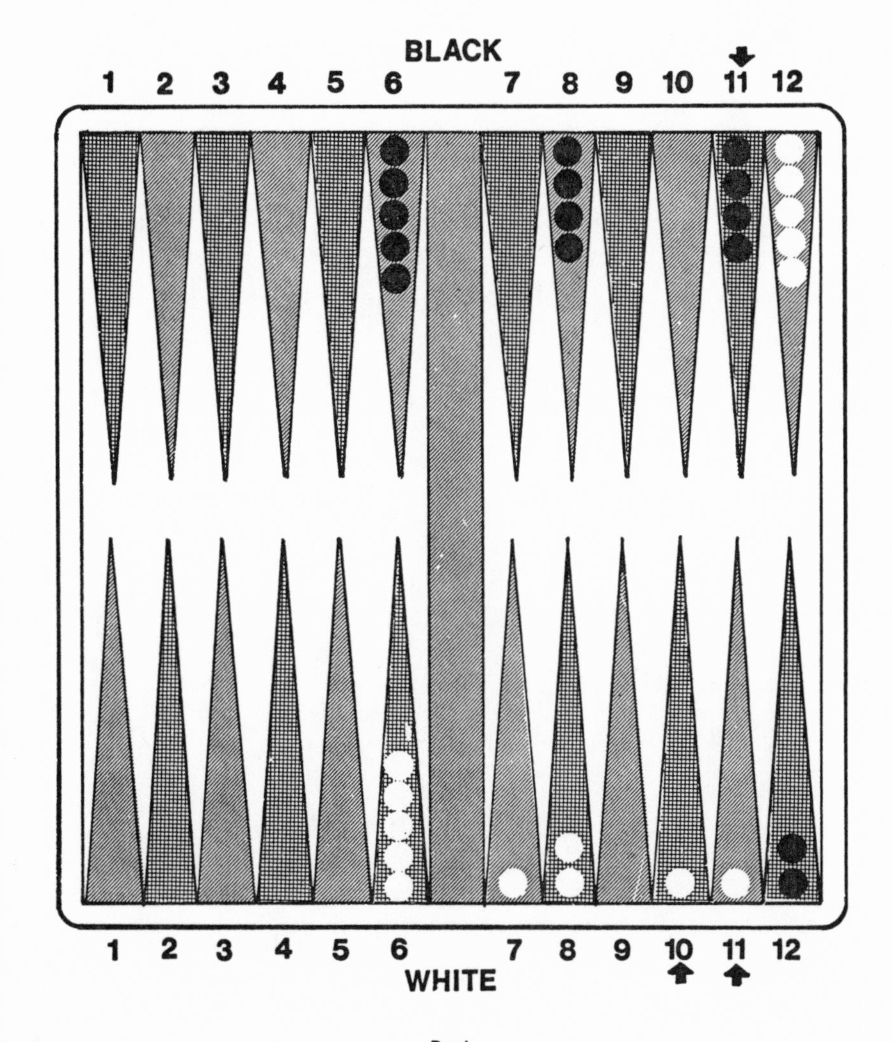

R–4

to 10–B and 11–B, leaving the board as shown in Diagram R–5.

This makes it utterly and officially a running game for both White and Black, with no possible way of altering that situation. At this stage, the game is very closely matched. To check that, you simply count the number of points each player has to roll to move all his stones to his inner table and bear them off from there. In this game, the count adds as follows:

White: 5 on his 6-point for 30; 2 on his 7-point for 14; 2 on his 8–point for 16; 1 on his 10 point; 1 on his 11-point

R–5

for 11; 4 on his 13-point (Black's 12-point) for 52. This gives White a total of 30 + 14 + 16 + 10 + 11 + 52 = 133.

Black: 5 on his 6-point for 30; 4 on his 8-point for 32; 1 on his 10-point for 10; 5 on his 11-point for 55. That gives Black a total of 30 + 32 + 10 + 55 = 127.

Since the average roll of a pair of dice is slightly over 8 points in backgammon (because of occasional doubles), this means that White should go out in 17 rolls, whereas Black should make it in 16 rolls. The edge, however, is in White's favor, since White has the first roll, a very potent factor in backgammon. So one or the other will come in first and win by a hair's breadth, which is not really enough to matter because:

In backgammon, you hope to take your opponent for a "gammon," which counts double, or a "backgammon," which counts triple. But you aren't likely to do either if you both go for a neck-to-neck running game, like the quickie just cited. Of course, if that occurs, some players attribute it to the roll of the dice or the luck of the game. They somehow fail to realize that though they can't control the dice, they can use the rolls toward shaping the game to come. What seems a trifling choice at the outset may have a great effect on what follows.

By way of comparision, suppose that in the case just detailed, the two players had given up thoughts of a running game and had gone for a blocking game instead, or had been forced into it. What could have happened will be shown next, using *the very same rolls* already given.

The Blocking Game

White opens with a roll of 6–5 and follows the standard procedure of moving a runner from 1–B to 12–B, a good start toward a running game. Black rolls 4–4, but can't see any advantage in trying to outrace White this early in the game. So Black moves two stones from 12–W to 5–B, thus making his own 5-point and establishing a block there. This leaves the board as shown in Diagram BL–1.

Black's block takes immediate effect when White rolls 5–4 and wants to move his second runner from 1–B to 10–B, only to find that he can't. Since Black has blocks on both 5–B and 6–B, White is unable to use either his 4 or his 5 as the first portion of his roll. So White moves two stones from 12–B; one to 8–W, the other to 9–W.

Black rolls 1–1, which proves very timely indeed. It enables him to move two stones from 6–B to 4–B, form-

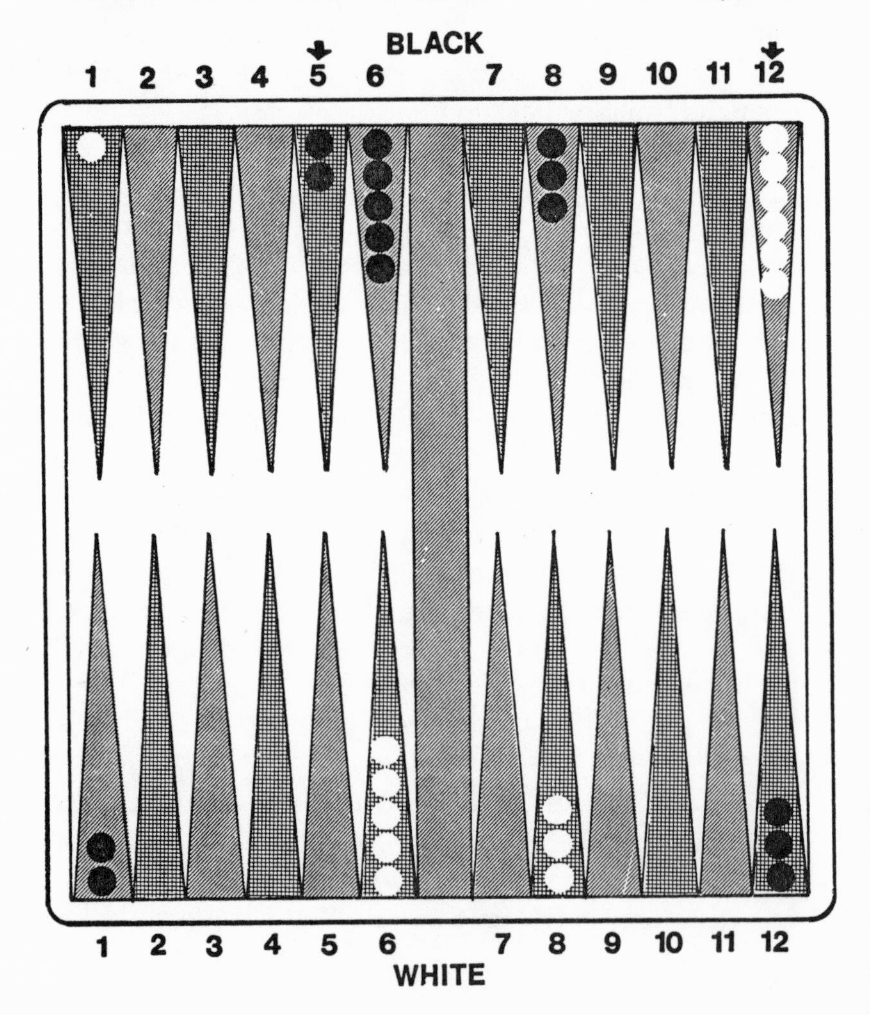

BL–1

ing three blocks in a row, on his 4-, 5-, and 6-points. With another on his 8-point, Black is well on his way toward establishing a prime, the big aim of every blocking game. The board now stands as shown in Diagram BL–2.

White rolls 2–1, which is trifling toward a running game, but helpful in a blocking game. So White decides to copy Black's tactics. White moves one stone from 9–W to 7–W, another from 8–W to 7–W, thus making his bar-point (7–W). Black comes through with a roll of 6–1 and moves one stone from 12–W to 7–B, another from 8–B to 7–B. Black thereby makes his bar-point (7–B), further

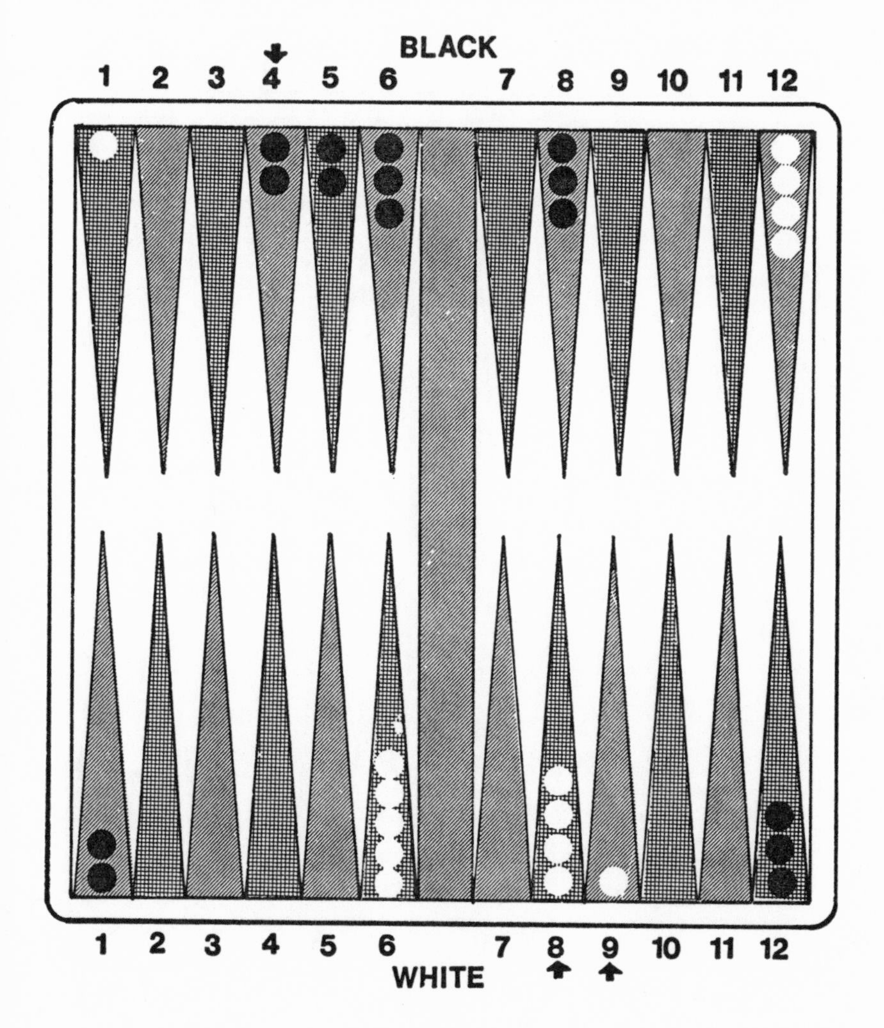

BL–2

strengthening his blocking game. That puts the board as shown in Diagram BL–3.

Only a 2–6 roll could enable White to bring his runner from 1–W past Black's blocks, as a last effort to resume a running game, if he still wants it. Instead, all that White rolls is a 3–2, so he moves one stone from 12–B to 10–W and another from 12–B to 11–W. This leaves two White blots, but Black would have to roll a 5–6 or a 6–6 to hit one. Black happens to roll something that he likes much better, a 2–2. With it, he abandons his comfort station on 12–W with a double move to 9–B, establishing his prime

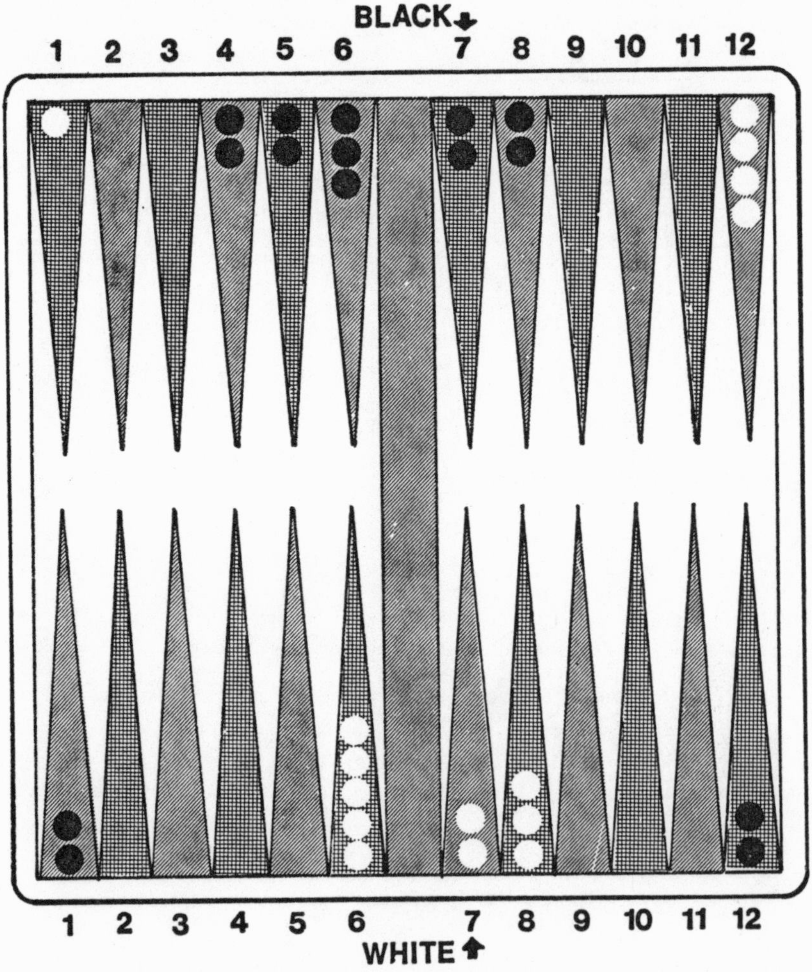

BL–3

of 6 points in a row. This is shown in Diagram BL–4.

White, with a roll of 5–1, presses toward a blocking game like Black's. White moves one stone from 10–W to 5–W, another from 6–W to 5–W, thus making his 5-point. Black rolls 3–2 and finds it timely indeed. Anything bigger might have disturbed Black's prime; but 3–2 enables him to bring one back man from 1–W to 4–W, another from 1–W to 3–W, putting both in a position to clear the hurdle of four White blocks. This is shown in Diagram BL–5.

White gets a nice roll of 4–2 and uses it to bring a stone from 12–B to 9–W and his blot from 11–W, where it was

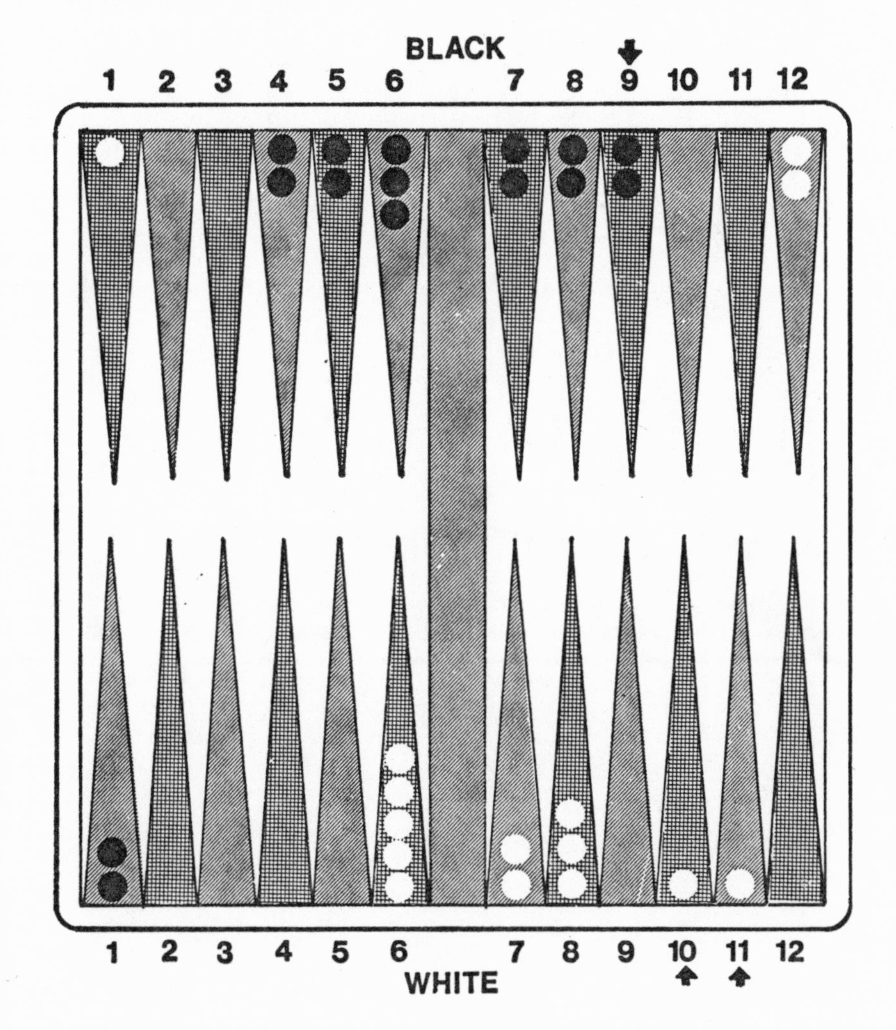

BL–4

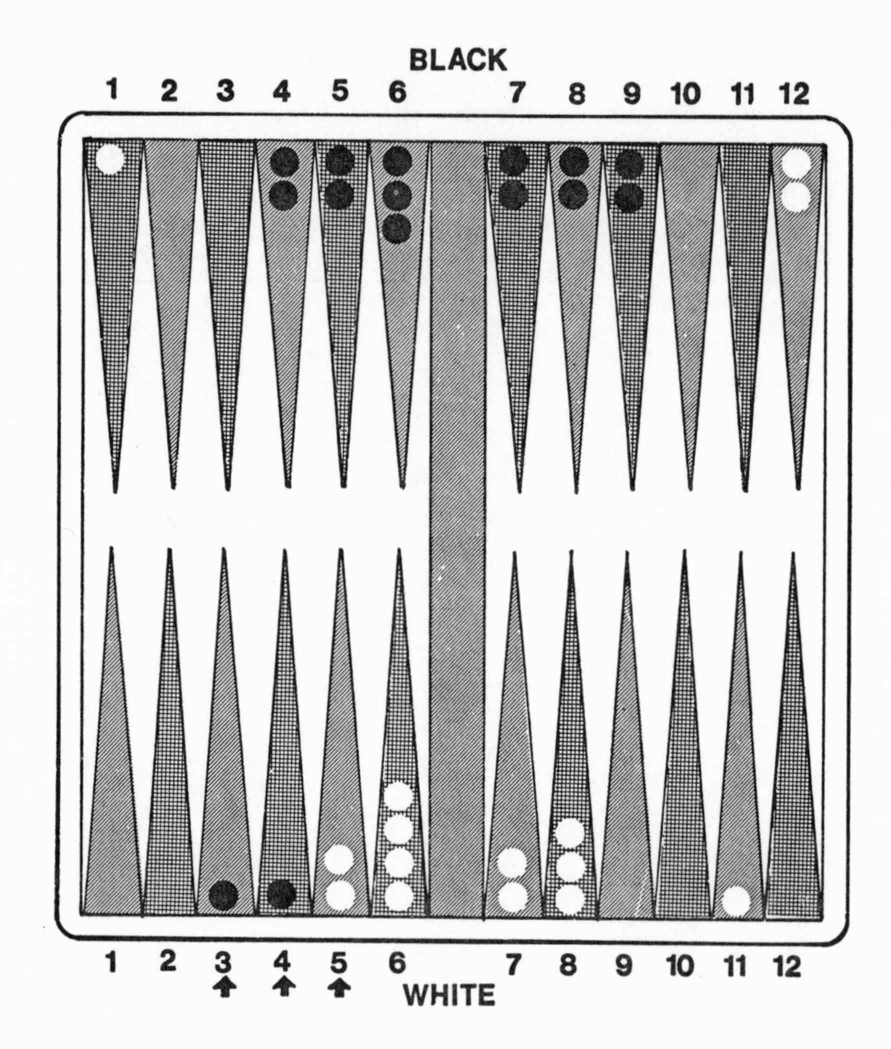

BL–5

quite vulnerable, to 9–W, where it enables White to make his 9-point. That leaves a White blot on 12–B, but the only way that Black can possibly hit it is with a roll of 6–3. Instead, Black rolls a 6–1 and uses it to move one back man from 4–W to 10–W the other from 3–W to 4–W, putting the board as shown in Diagram BL–6.

NOTE: In the rolls just described, White could have used his 4–2 to bring a stone from 8–W to 4–W and another from 6–W to 4–W, making his 4-point and hitting the Black stone there. But he preferred to bring stones from farther away, rather than clutter his inner table too soon.

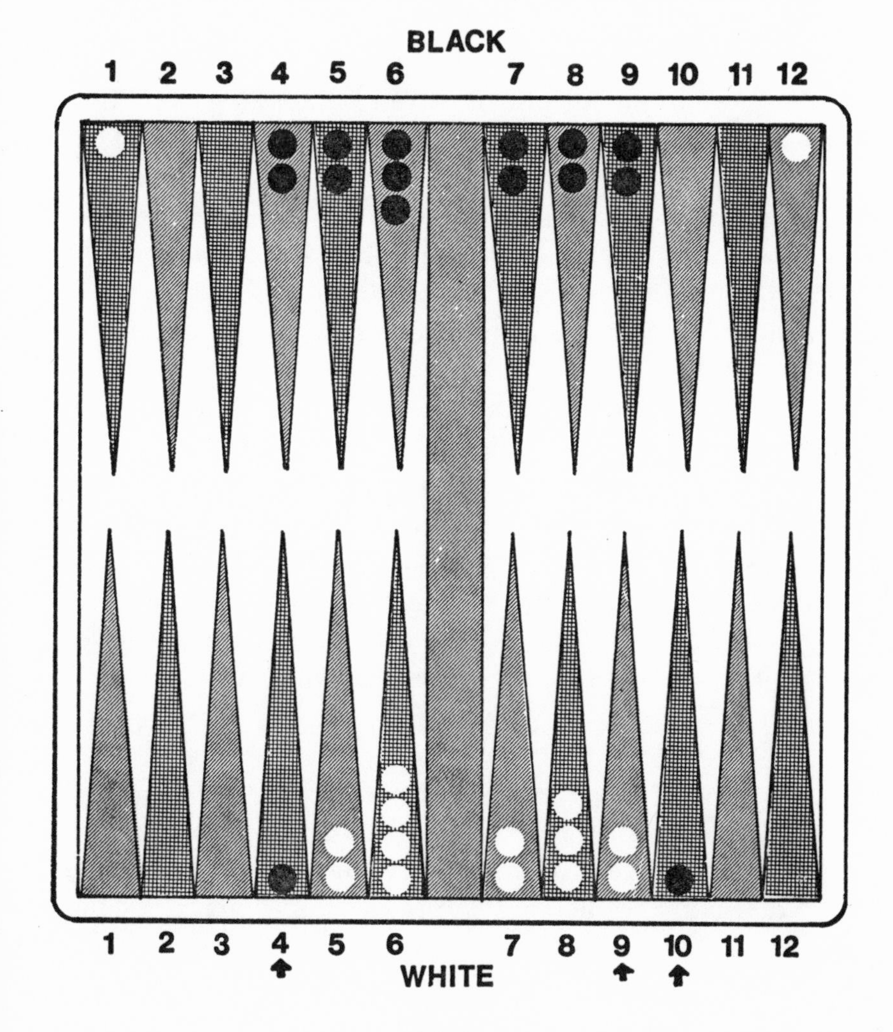

BL–6

White gets another 4–2, enabling him to do what he could have done on the last. He moves one stone from 8–W to 4–W and another from 6–W to 4–W, hitting the black blot and sending it to the bar. White makes his 4-point and with it, establishes a prime. If White had rolled a 3, either as a single die, or as 2–1, he could have hit the Black blot on 10–B and sent it to the bar. But White is running less risk of having his own blot on 12–B hit by Black. To do that, Black would have to roll a 1, 2, or 3 to reenter from the bar; and with it a 3 to move from 10–W to 12–B for the hit.

As it happens, Black rolls a 1–4, which he finds very helpful. He uses the 1 to reenter on 1–W; then applies the 4 to move his blot from 10–W to 11–B, passing the White blot on 12–B. This produces the situation shown in Diagram BL–7, with the players about equal. Each has a lone back man hemmed in by an opposing prime, so each has a Blocking game functioning perfectly—for the moment. But in order to bear off, either White or Black must first free his lone runner and bring him clear around to the home table.

This is a far cry from the climax of the running game, where it was just a question of which could clear his inner table more rapidly. Here, with both players blocked, each will have to break his prime in order to fulfill the moves required by his rolls. That may free the opposing back man prematurely; and even worse, it may become an imminent threat to any blot that a player is forced to leave while crowding some of his points too heavily.

Where Luck Enters

It is generally agreed that if two capable backgammon players lock horns in a contest, the outcome should prove very close, except when luck especially favors one or the other; and the dice are the factor that determines the

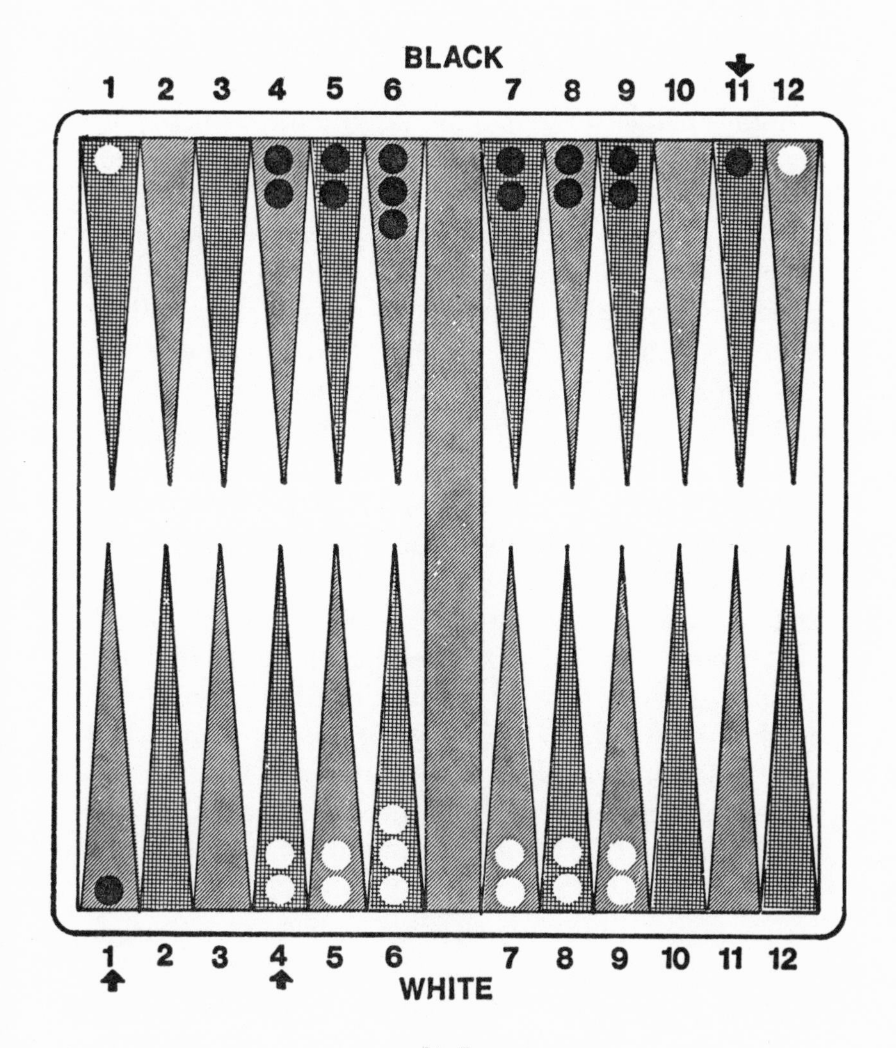

BL–7

luck. That was true in the old days when that saying was first promulgated, because then even the experts adhered to one objective, to "play it safe." That gives preference to the blocking game, rather than the running game, not so much to stop the opponent's advance, as to prevent your own stones from being hit.

A study of the backgammon board shows that both players are engaged in a blocking game to start, having been "given" certain points, instead of having to "make" them. The points originally allotted to a player are his own 6- and 8-points, with his opponent's 1- and 12-points; and these are so valuable that if a player gets just the rolls he wanted, mostly doubles, he might move to an easy victory, preserving his blocking game intact.

However, once a player is forced to leave blots, he is engaged in a running game, at least until he can bring up builders and form blocks. So the modern trend is to accept the risk and turn it to advantage; leaving early blots can pay big dividends if an opponent either is unable to hit them or passes up the opportunity because he belongs to the "play safe" school and is afraid to hit for fear of being hit back. However, once a blot is hit, retaliation is the quickest way to rectify the loss, so modern players frequently become involved in a "battle of blots" that may put one contestant so far ahead that his opponent has little hope of catching up through a running game or of impeding his opponent's progress with the usual blocking game. That is where a new element arises in the form of the back game, and although the odds are usually against its succeeding, it can sometimew accomplish results when all other measures would fail.

The Back Game

Professor Louis Hoffmann, noted British authority on backgammon of a century ago, summed the subject of the back game with this simple but succinct statement: "A player should never start, at the outset, with the intention of playing a back game, but he should be awake to any circumstances that may render it desirable to do so." That advice is as good today as ever, but it still leaves a question as to how soon the prospect of a back game may actually manifest itself.

Basically, a back game has been defined as "the strategy of not advancing runners early, but of using them to catch adverse blots when the opponent is well advanced." That, however tells only half the story. A player has two back men to start, but merely to lag with those until they become hopelessly boxed, would be no game at all. Indeed, some experts claim that the back men should be pulled out at the first opportunity, like wisdom teeth, being just about as unnecessary. All that is true, if you intend to play a running game and nothing else. With a blocking game, those back men may prove useful, while if you ever intend to play a back game, they may become essential, because:

By fuller definition, a back game is one wherein a player endeavors to offset a losing game, by placing four or more back men on his opponent's inner table, at the same time "making" at least two of the points. Again, Professor Hoffmann stands out as a pioneer in this department, for he advises holding the adversary's 1- and 2-points, or else his 1- and 3-points. These are still the best choices, and Hoffmann also recommends holding an extra man on the 1-point, so it can be used to hit opposing blots, leaving two back men still in control of the 1-point. That is still good today and modern players sometimes go it one better by using six back men to cover three points on the adversary's inner table.

Now, since a player has only two back men to start, it is obvious that the additional two, three, or four back men can only be the result of blots that have been hit and reentered from the bar. So if he starts by turning his two back men into runners and getting them clear of his adversary's inner table, he will have to set up two more blots and have them hit before he can go after a back game position. By then it may be too late, for his other stones may be too far advanced to make a back game feasible.

To recognize the factors governing the back game, revert to the sample game shown in Chapter 2 and note what happened after White split his back men and tried to turn them into runners beginning with his eighth roll (Diagram 8–A). Black not only hit the lead runner, but also hit a blot that White had been forced to leave on point 12–B; and to top that, Black later hit a blot that White had unwisely failed to cover on White's own 1-point. This was Black's eleventh roll (Diagram 11) and the crux of the situation came on White's next roll (Diagram 11–A).

There, White made a prompt reentry on 1–B, by using the 1 of a 1–5 roll. That gave him blocks on Black's 1-point and 3-point, a fine setup for a back game. But White preferred to continue his running game, using his 5 to move from 3–B to 8–B, (as shown in Diagram 11–A) and there White's blot was hit (Diagram 12) and White was unable to regain his block on Black's 3-point, as Black later "made" it for himself. So White, by staying with his running game, was unable to clear Black's blocks and therefore lost his chance for a back game.

Here is how White would have stood if he had tried a back game. Instead of moving from 3–B to 8–B, he would have moved from 6–W to 1–W, hitting the Black blot, as shown in diagram B-G-X.

Now, if you take the *very same rolls* that were made in the original game, you will find some interesting results, as follows:

Black rolls 1–3. Enters on 1–W, hitting a White blot.

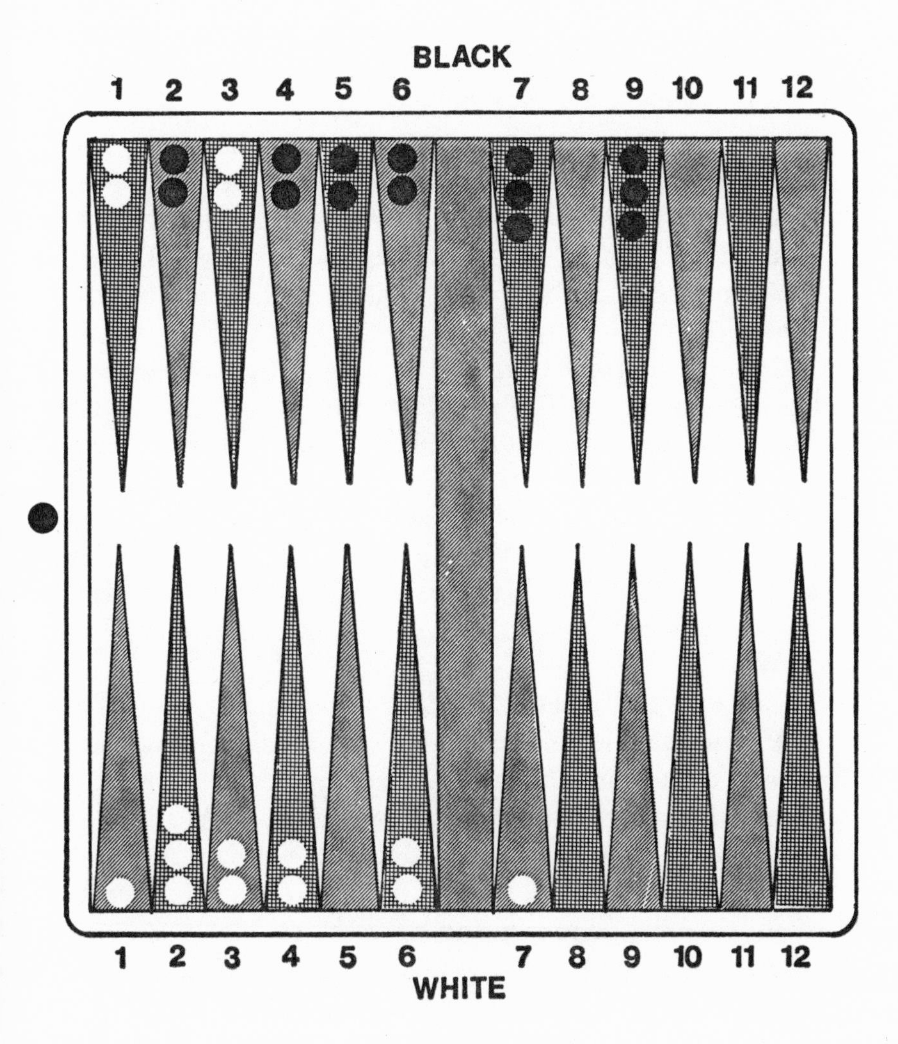

BGX

Black moves from 9–B to 6–B.

White rolls 4–2. Can't reenter.

Black rolls 5–4. Moves 9–B to 4–B; 9–B to 5–B.

Here, it is assumed that Black overlooked his opportunity to count his roll as 4–5, which would have enabled him to bring his runner from 1–W and on to 10–W.

White rolls 6–5. Can't reenter.

Since White can't move, White is keeping his own blockers intact on his own inner table, where the four points that he has made (2–W, 3–W, 4–W, 6–W) may delay Black from getting his runner loose from 1–W. But all Black needs is another break as good as the one he overlooked.

The break comes when Black rolls 6–3 and moves his back man from 1–B to 7–B, hitting the White blot on 7–B and continuing on to 10–B. That puts two of White's stones on the bar, which means that he will have to reenter both, before he can move to impede Black's progress. But White does that on the very next roll with a 1–1. This double enables him to reenter both stones from the bar on 1–B and to move two from 6–W to 5–W.

The board now stands as shown on the opposite page:

If Black should roll low and White should produce a 5 or a 6, White could bring out a back man from 3–B to try and hit Black's runner coming home from 10–W. White's best roll, of course, would be a 2–5 or a 2–6, as it would enable him to bring a surplus back man from Black's 1-point (1–B) while preserving his block on Black's 3-point (3–B).

As it actually happened, Black rolled a high 6–4, which enabled him to bring his runner from 10–W to 5–B, joining the Black blockers already on that point.

From then on, White was fighting a losing cause, but a lucky break could have turned the tide his way. If

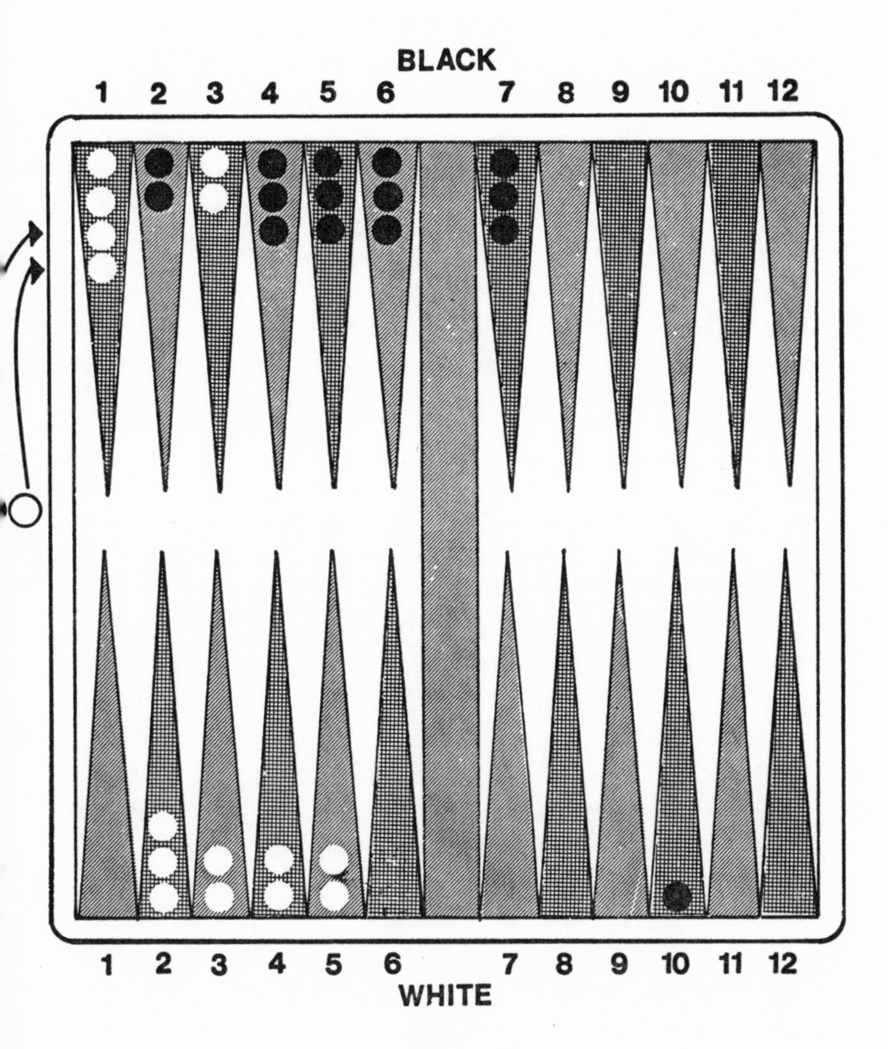

BGY

White could free those surplus back men on 1–B and bring them home with low rolls while Black began bearing off his stones, Black might be forced to leave a blot for White to hit. By then, White would have two new blockers joining those on his inner board, making it harder for Black to reenter.

Going back to the original situation (Diagram 11), it is apparent that White could have done better to stay with his running game by risking a blot, despite the fact that his roll gave him four back men on the two best points for a back game. That part was fine; the flaw lay in the fact that White's running game had gone too far, leaving his runners too advanced for a good back game, in which the player should be well back and sometimes a long way back. The way to determine that is to count the needed points. That can be done very quickly, by following the simple formula proposed by Edmond Hoyle, a century before Professor Hoffmann. It is this:

The player counts all the stones on his inner table at 1 point each; those on his outer table at 2 each; those on his opponent's outer table at 3 each; those on his opponent's inner table at 4 each. Any stones on the bar are included with those on the inner table. Now in this case, if White had followed the original Hoyle formula, instead of going along with modern fads, he would have summed it thus:

When White established his back game (as shown in Diagram B-G-X) he should have counted his score and Black's. If he had, it would have totaled thus:

White:		Black:	
inner table	10	inner table	8
outer table	2	outer table	12
opposing outer table	0	opposing outer table	0
opposing inner table	16	opposing inner table	4
	28		24

Horrors! White is 4 points behind Black! So White should go into a back game. Far from it. Things are so nearly equal that they practically cancel out. So White shouldn't have gone along with the back game. But there are many times when White—or Black—should. If they want to know when, the good old Hoyle count will tell them. Suppose that the layout had been somewhat different, as shown in the diagram below:

From White's standpoint, his four back men, holding Black's 1- and 3-points, spell out the same message: "Go for a back game." An average player might have gone

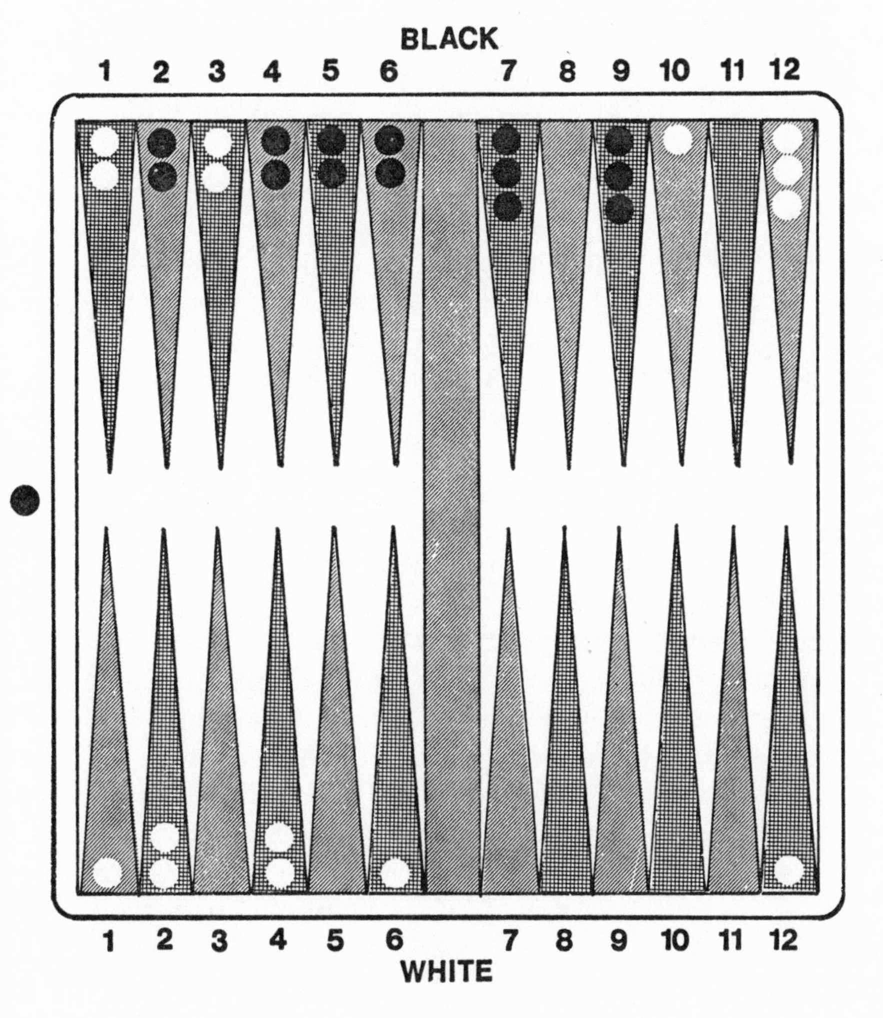

along with it, without calculating further. But actual calculation, according to Hoyle, certifies the urge for a back game, as follows:

White's inner table	6	Black's inner table	8
White's outer table	2	Black's outer table	12
opposing outer table	12	opposing outer table	0
opposing inner table	16	blot on bar	4
Total	36		24

That difference should not only invite a back game, it should provoke it. White has little or no chance of getting those back men free before Black reenters and brings his runner home, with the six men on his outer board (from 7–B and 9–B). But then, White can start sniping off Black blots, while Black is bearing off.

Assuming that it is Black's roll, if Black rolls 1–5, he can enter on 1–W and move to 6–W, hitting two White blots, giving Black's runner a chance to get home while White is reentering them, but that can prove to White's advantage if he reenters soon enough to bring some of his own men home and make points on his own inner table to block reentry of those future Black blots.

If Black prefers, he can reenter on 1–W and move a blocker from 9–B to 4–B, sending only one White blot to the bar. Or he could get the same result by reentering on 5–W and hitting the White blot on 6–W, sending it to the bar instead. This would give White only one new back man instead of two, which Black might feel was to his own advantage. By that same token, Black might consider it better to enter on 5–W and move a blocker from 7–B to 6–B, without hitting any White blots. What then?

In that case, White would have a roll coming. He could hit the Black blot on 5–W with a 1 from a single die, by moving from 6–W to 5–W: or with a total roll of 7, from 12–W; or a total of 8, from 12–B; or a total of 10 from 10–B.

This would force Black to reenter his runner, this time with White blots waiting to be hit on 1–B, 5–B and 6–B.

Suppose, however, that White should come up with a roll like 4–2, giving him no chance of hitting the Black blot on 5–W. What should White do then? Just this: he should deploy two blockers from 12–B by moving them to 9–W and 11–W, thus turning them into blots. The board would then appear as shown below:

It's Black's roll and look what confronts him now! If he rolls a 1, or has a total of 4, 6, 7, 8, or 10 he will have to hit a White blot with his runner from 5–B, or keep it

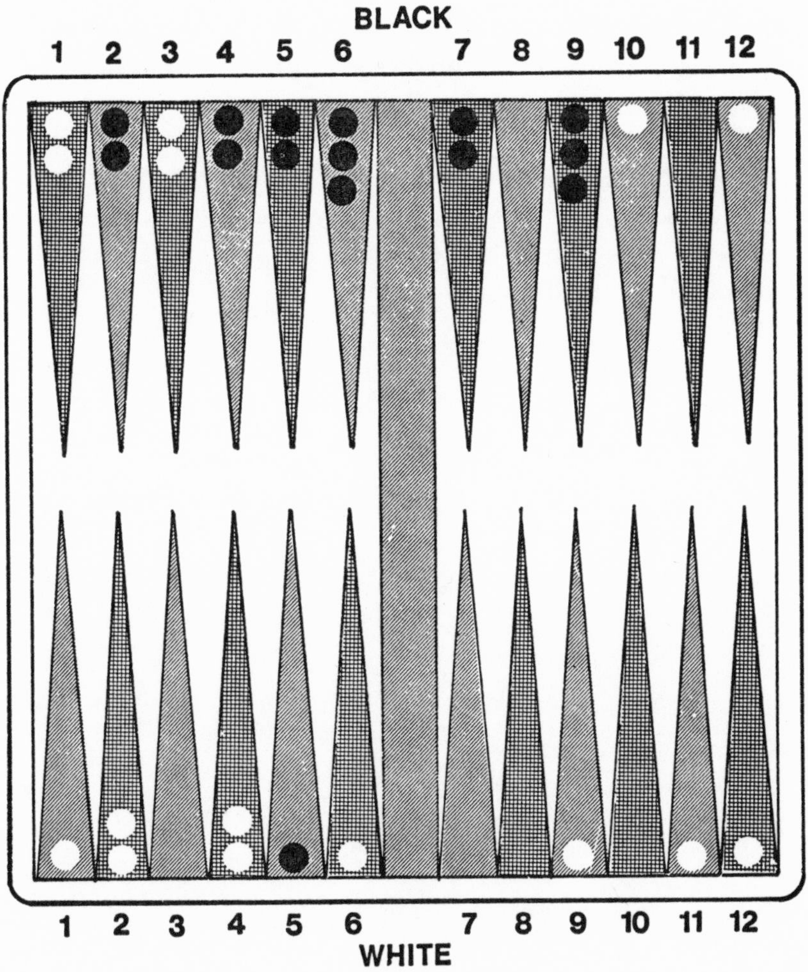

BLACK

1 2 3 4 5 6 7 8 9 10 11 12

1 2 3 4 5 6 7 8 9 10 11 12

WHITE

BGZ–2

where it is. A single 6 on one die would be most embarrassing, because the only stone that Black could move would be his blot, as a survey of the board will show.

There are some helpful rolls, of course. With a 3–1, Black could keep his blot on 5–W and move a blocker from 9–B to 5–B. But it would then be White's turn; and all White would need to roll would be a 4, 6 on a single die, or a total roll of 4, 6, 7, 8, or 10 to hit the Black blot and force Black to reenter it again, with the same committee of White blots waiting to be hit and hit back. If White can keep picking off Black's runner while gaining another back man of his own, he may make sufficient points on his inner table to block the reentry of other Black blots that White's back men may be lucky enough to hit; and from there, White may turn his back game into a winner.

Summarized, the back game is loaded with intriguing prospects, that can only be appreciated by testing them out, either in practice or actual play. But as a bet, the back game is definitely a long shot and anyone embarking on it should keep that fact in mind.

V

Bearing Off

AS SPECIFIED EARLIER, THE FIRST OBJECTIVE IN BACKgammon is for a player to bring all of his stones into his inner table, so that he can fulfill the second and final objective, that of bearing them off and winning the game. Here, a beginner is apt to encounter trouble by being overeager to bring stones home to his inner table, with the result that he crowds too many on the lower points instead of making up a well-distributed table.

If White is bringing stones to his inner table while Black still has two blockers on White's 3-point (3–W), it is obvious that any stones that White moves on to his 1- or 2-points (1–W and 2–W) will be wasted so far as containing Black's back men is concerned. White may soon find himself short of stones on his 4-, 5- and 6-points, making it easier for Black to turn his blockers into runners and escape; or even worse, Black may hit a blot that White is forced to leave on one of these vital points and thus stop White from bearing off.

Naturally, a few stones on the lower points are helpful, as they can be borne off cheaply whenever their owner rolls a 1 or 2 and others can be moved in later to supplant them, if need be. White should be careful, however, to keep an even number of men on the 5- and 6-points combined, as a throw of double 6 or double 5 might force him to leave a blot when bearing off from those points, giving Black a chance for a hit with one of his lurking back men.

Preparing to Bear Off

Sometimes, even in the early stages of a forward game, a player finds that he can often make almost any move he wants, without unduly risking his blots being hit. That is when he should give special attention to making the most of his rolls, with the idea of getting all of his stones on to his home board as soon as possible, so that he can start bearing off ahead of his opponent. Hence, the fewer moves needed to accomplish that aim, the better off the player will be. So he should watch for opportunities to reach certain key points that are a help to speedy progress.

Taking the situation from Black's standpoint, we find that Black, at the very outset, has two runners on the first of these key points; that is, point 1–W. From there, a roll of a single 6 can carry a Black runner to the next key, which is White's bar-point, 7–W. The reason that both are keys is that that single 6 brings a Black runner from the lowest point of White's inner table (1–W) to the lowest point of White's outer table (6–W).

Black can sometimes do this at the very outset of the game, but after that it becomes difficult, as one of White's main objectives is to make his bar-point, by putting two or more men on 7–W, thus preventing Black from using it as a key point toward his own advance. Also, it is generally risky for Black to move his runners too early, but as the game progresses it becomes imperative to put them

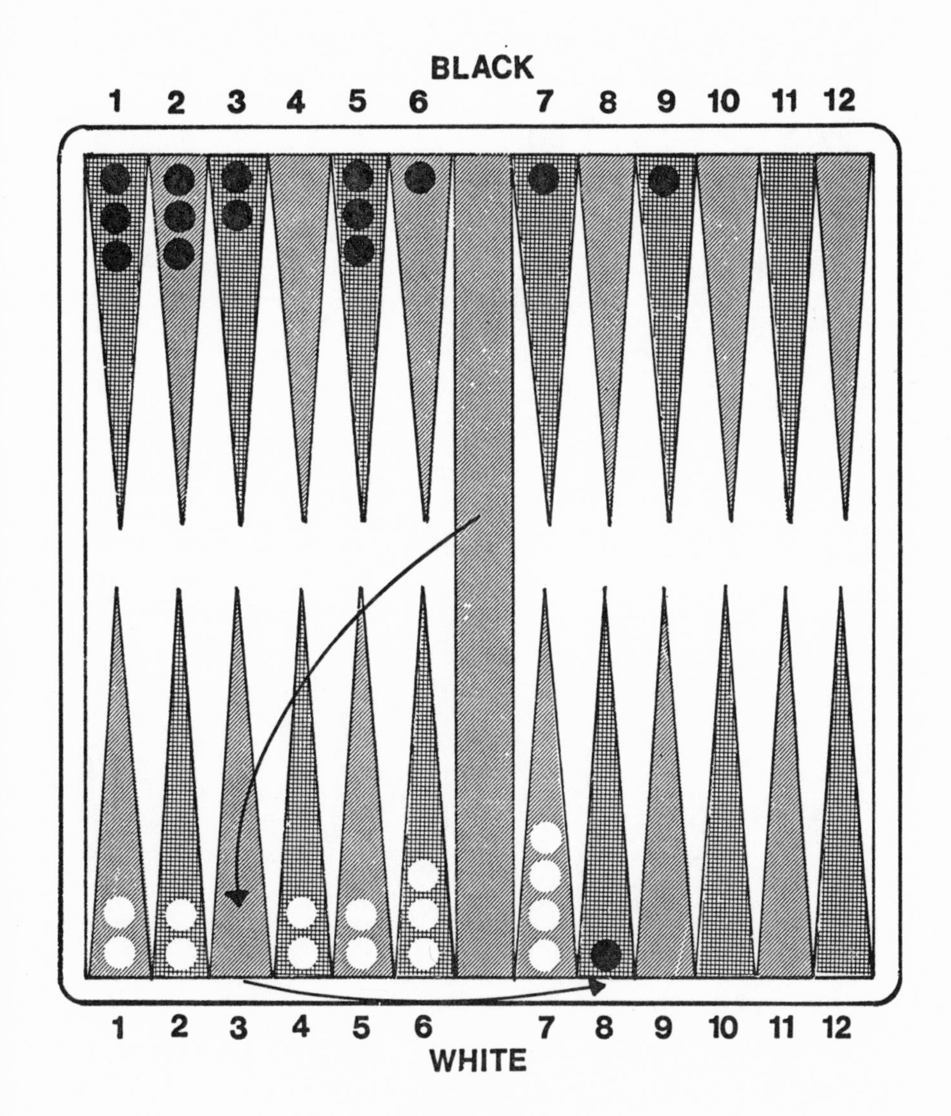

DIAGRAM 1

(See pages 132 and 134)

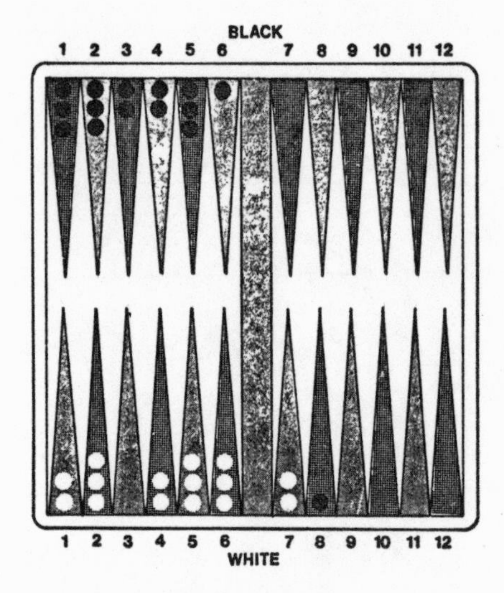

DIAGRAM 2

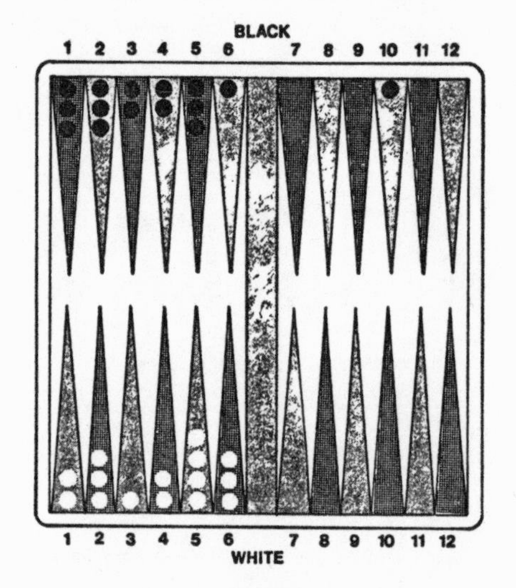

DIAGRAM 3

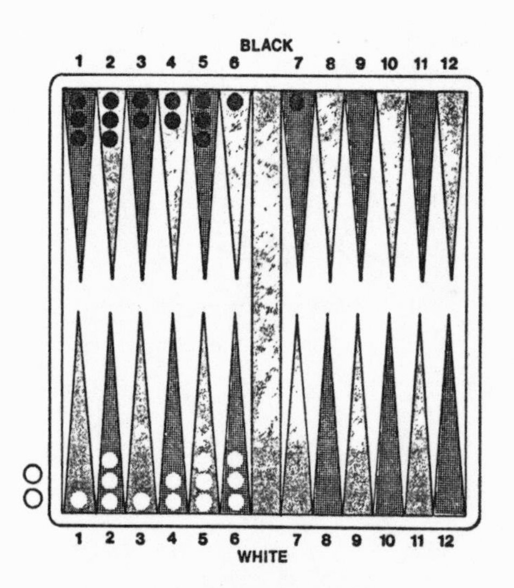

DIAGRAM 4

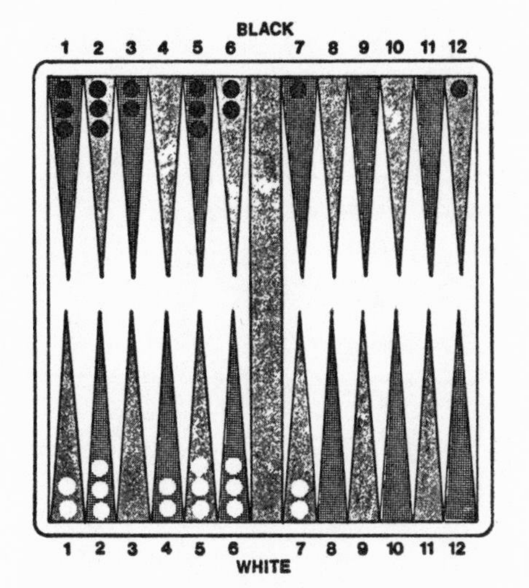

DIAGRAM 5

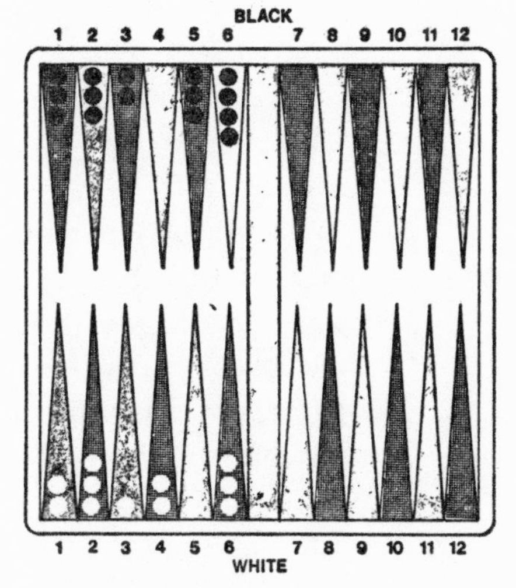

DIAGRAM 6

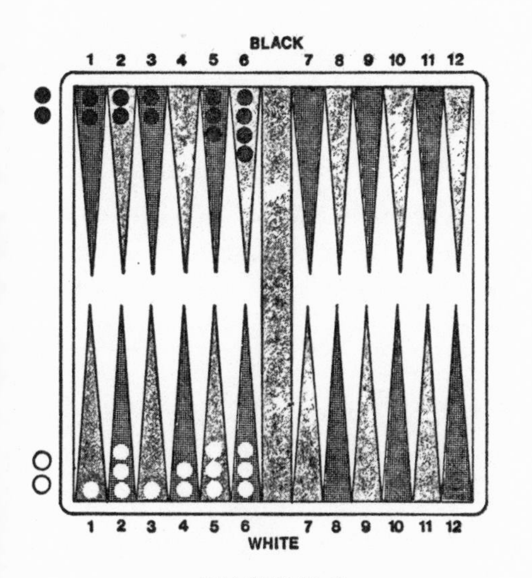

DIAGRAM 7

into action, particularly when it reaches the status of a running game where both Black and White are racing to get men home first.

This also applies when Black reenters stones that have been sent to the bar. If they can't make it exactly to 7–W (White's bar-point—particularly if White is firmly fixed there—Black may be able to move beyond it, with 8–W serving as a good substitute key if it happens to be unoccupied by White. The next key, from Black's standpoint, is 12–B, which can be reached by a single 6 from 7–W or by a 5 from 8–W. That puts Black on his own outer table and from 12–B another roll of 6 will carry him to his own 6-point (6–B) which puts him on his own inner table. When the time comes, he can bear off from that point with a single roll of 6, so Black's 6-point (6–B) becomes his final key.

A smart player will begin thinking in terms of keys much sooner than his opponent suspects; in fact, some opponents do not think about keys at all, which is why they lose so many games of backgammon. To illustrate this clearly and at the same time emphasize the important part that key points can play toward bringing home a winner, the following brief example will suffice. It represents a close approach to the end of a running game. To make its message ring clear, it will first be described as Black *shouldn't* have played it; then as Black *should* have played it.

The Wrong Way

The board stands as shown in Diagram 1. White has brought eleven stones home and has four more on his 7-point (7–W) but has left his 3-point (3–W) open, which was lucky for Black, because he had a stone on the bar and had to reenter it in order to stay in the game. Fortunately, he rolled a 3–5 on his turn and reentered on 3–W, moving from there to 8–W, as shown in the diagram. That took Black clear out of danger, making it a pure running game from there on. But White has an advantage, in that he is sure of getting all four stones home from 7–W in his next two rolls, while Black may have trouble gaining the same result.

This is what happened:

White rolled 5–2 and moved one stone from 7–W to 2–W; another from 7–W to 5–W, bringing two stones to his home board. Black responded with a 5–3, and to show White that he was just as good or better, Black moved one stone from 9–B to 4–B and another from 7–B to 4–B. In so doing, Black made his 4-point (4–B), establishing a block there, though he didn't need it at this late stage of the game. However, it made his board look very nice, as you can see from Diagram 2.

It was White's turn now and he rolled 4–2, so he moved a stone from 7–W to 3–W and another from 7–W to 5–W. Black then rolled the bones, hoping for a bigger total. He got it, 6–1, but it wasn't as big as he wanted. Black used it to move his lone stone from 8–W to 10–B, as shown in Diagram 3.

White was now ready to bear off, so he couldn't miss, having stones on all the points in his home table (6–W to 1–W inclusive). White rolled 5–1 and bore off one stone from 5–W and another from 1–W. But when Black rolled, hoping for a big one, he caught the worst possible result, a 2–1. All Black could do was move his lone stone from 10–B to 7–B, which left him short of his home table (Diagram 4).

As a result, White was able to bear off two more stones on his next roll, giving him four in all, while Black still had to bring in the stone from 7–B and therefore was able to bear off only one. On the next roll, White was almost sure to bear off two more, putting him five ahead of Black. Although Black still had a roll coming up, he would be in a bad spot unless he could roll a high double, or perhaps a couple of them. Otherwise, he would be out of the running, all because he ignored key plays.

The Right Way

Going back to the original position (Diagram 1), it is possible to study the results of *the same rolls,* if Black used them in an efficient way, with key points as his targets. White rolls 5–2 and makes his only possible moves of 7–W to 2–W and 7–W to 5–W. Black, however, uses the 5 of his 5–3 to move his most remote stone from 8–W to the next key point of 12–B. He also uses his 3 to move from 9–B to 6–B. The result of this 100 percent efficient play is shown in Diagram 5.

On the next roll, shown in Diagram 6, White uses his 4–2 roll to advance from 7–W to 3–W and 7–W to 5–W, bringing all his stones home. Black, in his turn, uses his 6–1 roll to move one stone from 12–B to 6–B and another from 7–B to 6–B, bringing both home by landing them on the same key point (6–B). That keeps Black squarely in the running, because:

When White rolls 5–1 and bears off from 5–W and 1–W, Black can use his untimely 2–1 to bear off from 2–B and 1–B, keeping him neck-and-neck with White, as shown in Diagram 7. White still is a roll ahead; but give Black a double roll, or a few big rolls, while White is getting small ones, and Black may come in winner.

Good Judgment in Bearing Off

A situation requiring good judgment in bearing off is shown on the board illustrated below, where White has brought all his stones to his inner table, with three on his ace-point, two each on his 3- and 4-points; three on his 5-point; and five on his 6-point. It is White's turn to roll and he is only slightly worried by the presence of the two Black stones on the 2-point. All the rest of Black's stones are already on his home table or on their way there, but White's advantage seems nearly insurmountable.

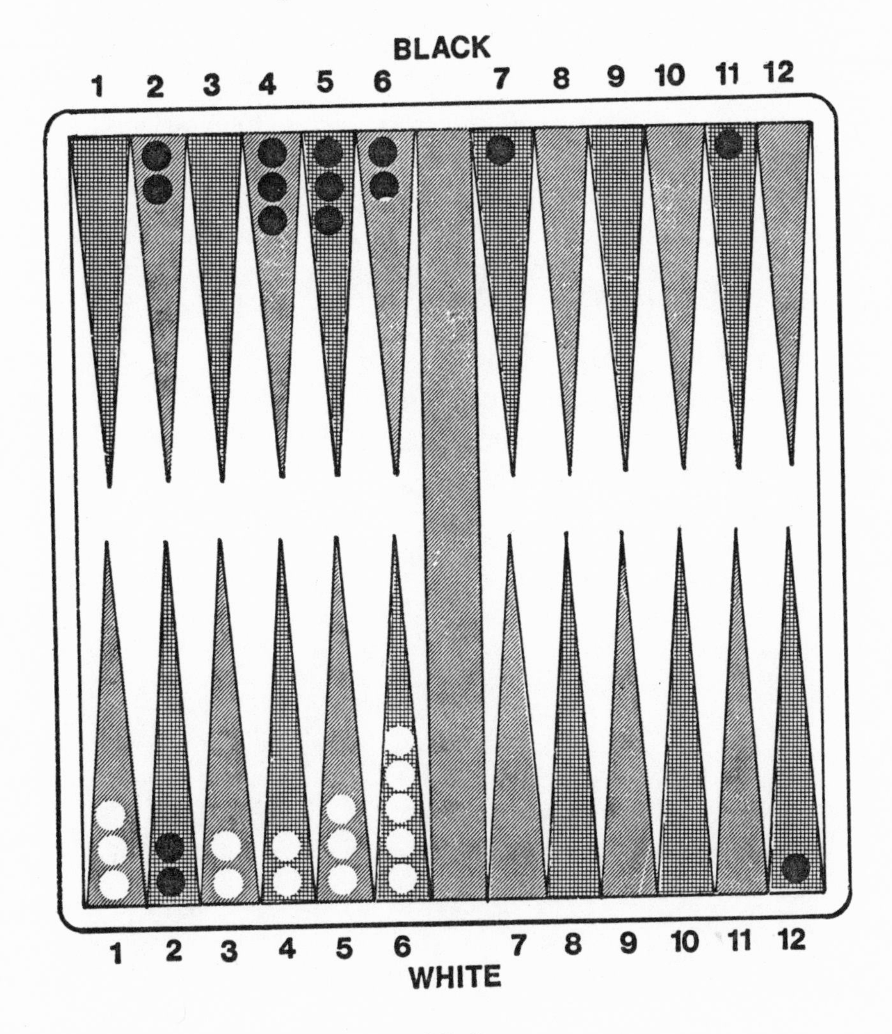

BO–1

Then White comes up with the best of all rolls under most circumstances, but in this case, the worst that he could possibly get, a double 6. By the rules, White must use all his roll if possible and his only way is to bear off four stones from his 6-point, leaving a blot there. As the board now stands, if Black rolls a 4 on either die, he can hit the blot with one of his back men and send it to the bar, from which White will be unable to reenter it for some time to come. Fortunately for White, Black rolls a 5–3 and uses it to move from W–12 to B–8 and from B–11 to B–8, so the status of White's home table remains unchanged.

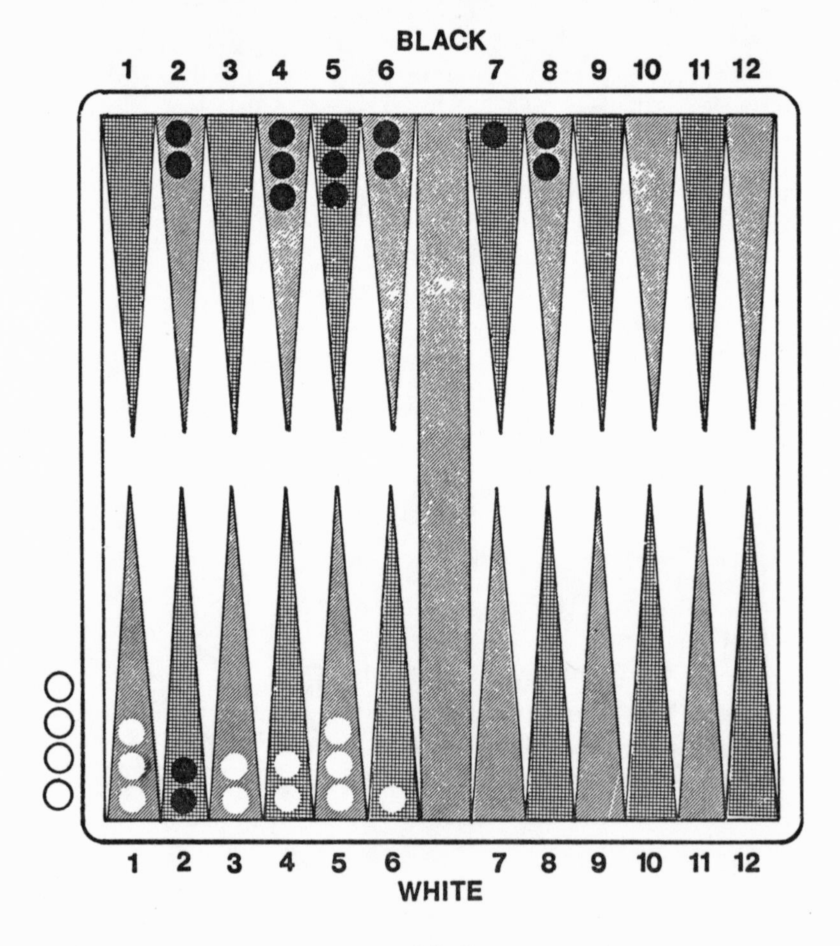

BO–2

Hoping for a better or safer roll, White comes up with 6–3, which puts him in a new dilemma. Again, he must use the 6 to its full extent, but if he bears off the blot from his 6-point, he will have to leave one elsewhere. He can't use his 3 to move from his 5-point to his 2-point, because Black has a block there. If he moves from his 4-point to his 1-point, he will leave a blot on his 4-point. If he bears off a stone from his 3-point, he will leave a blot there.

Where should White leave the blot—on his 3-point, where Black can hit it with a 1, or on his 4-point, where Black can hit it with a 2. It's one of those choices where whatever a player does may prove to be the wrong thing. Some would say that White should bear off from his 3-point, since that would mean one less stone to bear off later, but that doesn't help the problem enough to matter. The way to solve it is for White to take advantage of the two following rules:

First, it is permissible for a player to move either stone first, so White takes advantage of that rule by turning his 6–3 into a 3–6. He moves his troublesome blot, or lone stone, from his 6-point to his 3-point, utilizing his 3 for that purpose (Diagram 3). He then reverts to the second rule, which applies to bearing off; namely, that if a player rolls a number higher than any point occupied by any of his stones, he must bear off a stone from the highest occupied point. So in this case, he uses his 6 to bear off a stone from his 5-point, which is the highest point now occupied (Diagram 4).

This leaves the board as finally shown, with five stones borne off, three of White's stones on his ace-point, three more on his 3-point and two each on his 4- and 5-points. All are still safely held by White and his chances of bearing off his remaining stones successfully are very good, though there are still some rolls that might cause him trouble.

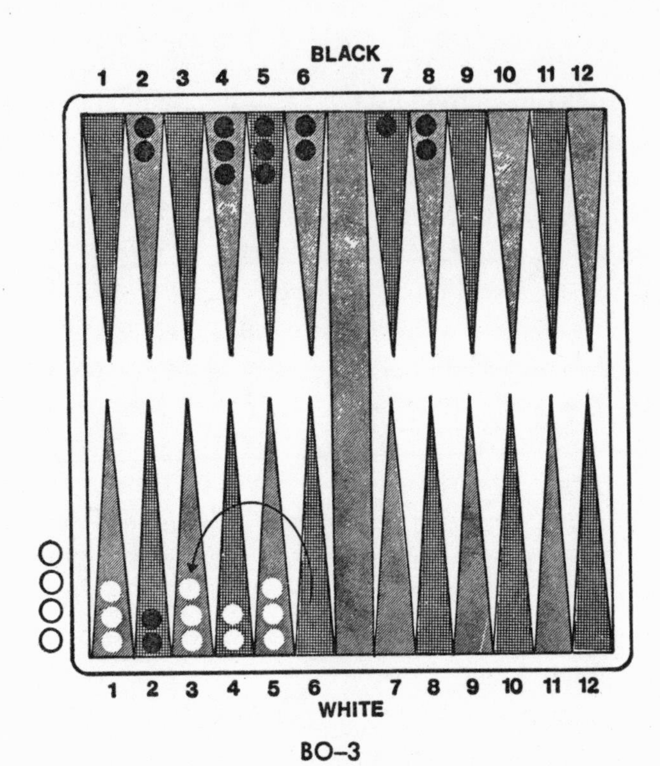

BO–3

BLACK

1 2 3 4 5 6 7 8 9 10 11 12

1 2 3 4 5 6 7 8 9 10 11 12

WHITE

BO–4

The Very Last Man

Here is a real tight situation that narrows a game down to the very last man. The board stands as shown below:

Black rolls a 6–2 and would ordinarily bear off from 5–B and 2–B. But Black makes a different move, as will be shown later. White rolls a 5–4 and bears off from W–3 and W–2, the only moves he can make. That leaves Black with three stones on the board, and ordinarily they would be on 2–B, 2–B, and 5–B. So Black

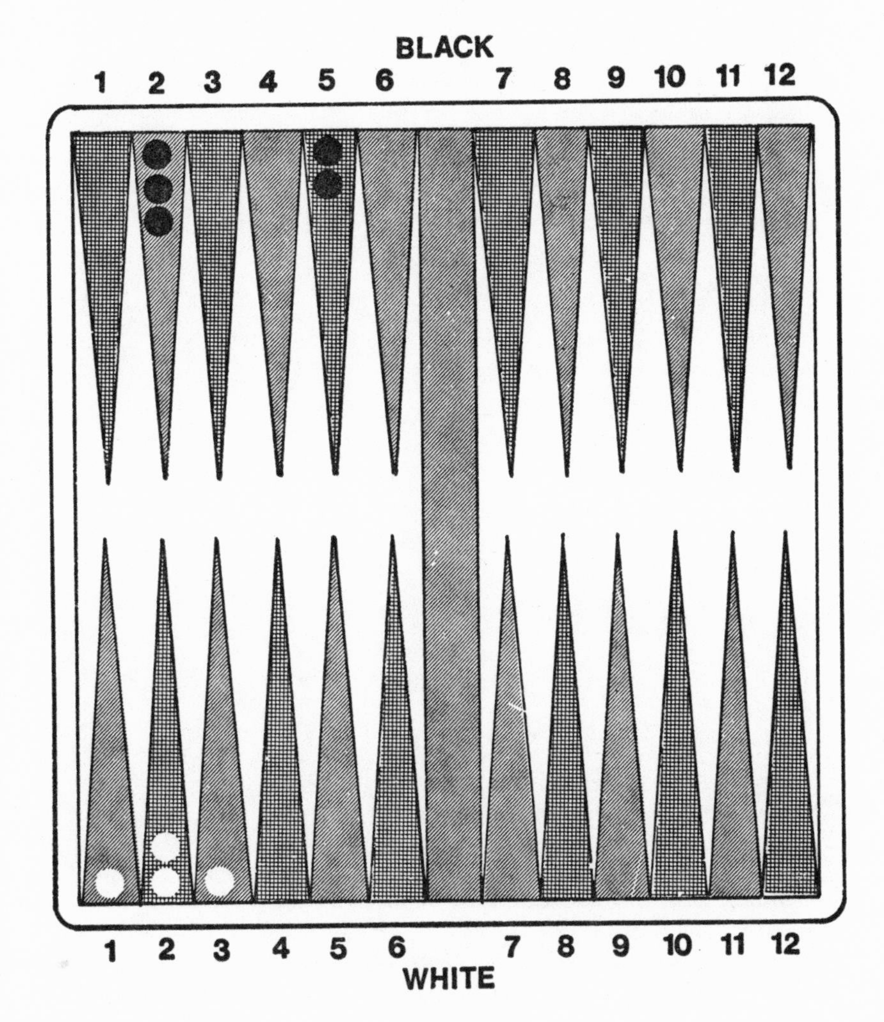

would have to throw a double 3, 4, 5 or 6 to bear off his three men before White wins the victory with any roll whatever.

But Black foresaw that and on his 6–2 roll, he only bore off a single stone, one of those on 5–B. He then moved the other from 5–B to 3–B, leaving three stones on 2–B. After White threw his 5–4 and bore off from 3–W and 2–W, the board stood as shown here:

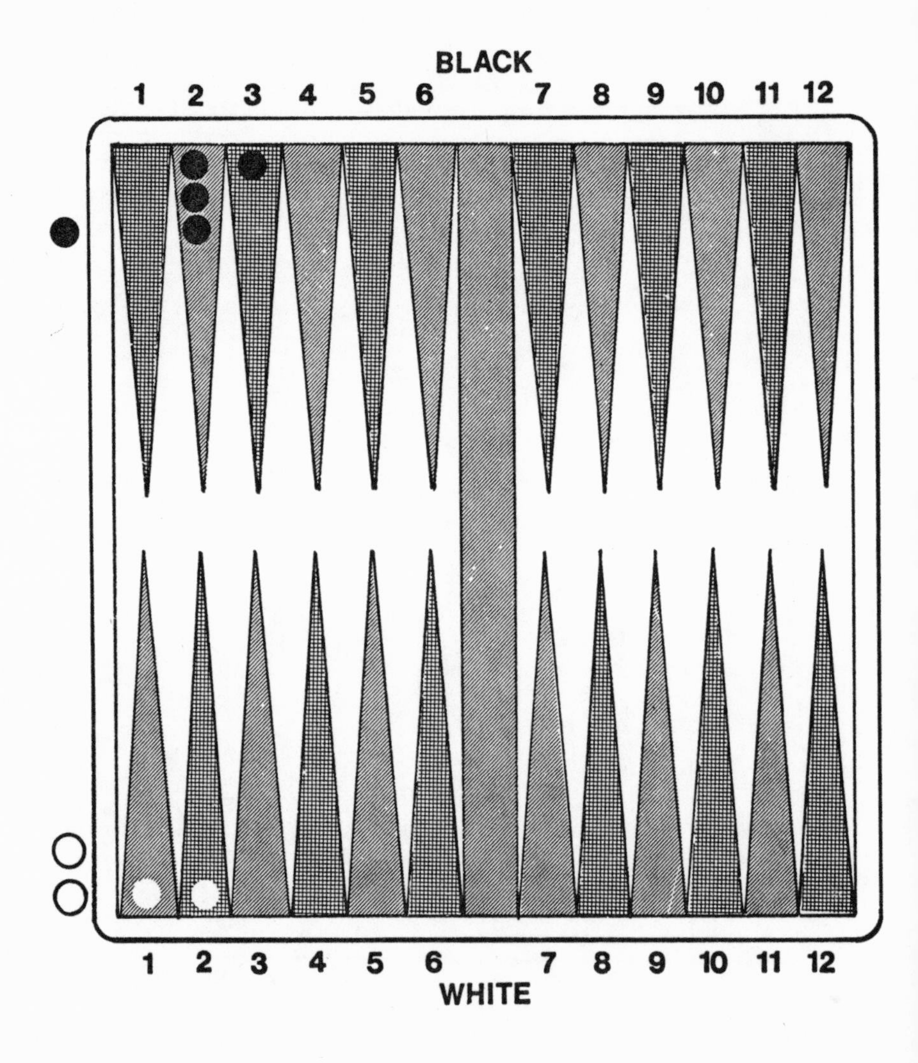

It is now Black's roll and he has quite as good a chance of winning as he would if he had left a stone on 5–B. A double roll will bear off four stones just as well as three; and with this setup, Black can make it with a double 3 or double 4, as well as a double 5 or double 6.

At times, you really have a better chance of bearing off four stones than only three. Go back to page 139, and give Black two stones on 5–B and three on 2–B. Suppose Black rolls a double 1 and bears off two stones from 2–B. (each $1 + 1 = 2$) That leaves two on 5–B and one on 2–B, so he must roll a double 5 or double 6 to bear off all three.

If, instead, he used his double 1 to bear off just one stone from 2–B, and used single points to move both stones from 5–B to 4–B, he would have two left on 4–B and two on 2–B. If he rolls a double 4, 5, or 6, he can bear off all his stones, so he has three possible rolls instead of only two. It is still a long shot, but that is the kind of foresight that brings home winners in backgammon.

Another neat caper: Black has just four stones, all on 6–B. He rolls double 6 and bears off one stone ($2 + 2 + 2 = 6$) and moves one from 6–B to 4–B. He then needs a double 6 on his next roll to bear off all three. But on his first roll of double 2, he could simply move all four stones from 6–B to 4–B, giving him three possible rolls—double 4, 5 or 6, that would bear them all off, instead of only double 6.

The 36 Possible Throws of the Dice

						1–6					
					1–5	2–5	2–6				
				1–4	2–4	3–4	3–5	3–6			
			1–3	2–3	3–3	4–3	4–4	4–5	4–6		
		1–2	2–2	3–2	4–2	5–2	5–3	5–4	5–5	5–6	
	1–1	2–1	3–1	4–1	5–1	6–1	6–2	6–3	6–4	6–5	6–6
Totals:	2	3	4	5	6	7	8	9	10	11	12

Number of Points a Player Can Move

Rolls	1	2	3	4	5	6	7	8	9	10	11	12	15	16	18	20	24
Singles	11	11	11	11	11	11	0	0	0	0	0	0	0	0	0	0	0
Pairs	0	1	2	3	4	5	6	5	4	3	2	1	0	0	0	0	0
Threes	0	0	1	0	0	1	0	0	1	0	0	1	1	0	1	0	0
Fours	0	0	0	1	0	0	0	1	0	0	0	1	0	1	0	1	1
Total Chances	11	12	14	15	15	17	6	6	5	3	2	3	1	1	1	1	1

Special Counts from Rolls of Doubles

Double I:	1–1–1	1–1–1–1	Double 4:	4–4–4	4–4–4–4
Double 2:	2–2–2	2–2–2–2	Double 5:	5–5–5	5–5–5–5
Double 3:	3–3–3	3–3–3–3	Double 6:	6–6–6	6–6–6–6

VI

Know Your Odds

THANKS TO THOSE EVER-ROLLING DICE, BACKGAMMON IS a game in which the odds play a major part and a player who studies those odds and uses them to good advantage can do much to counteract most of the so-called luck that also characterizes this grand old game. So far, the odds have been discussed chiefly in terms of opening moves, styles of games, bearing off, and various minor factors that have presented themselves for due consideration.

Even beginners are quick to appreciate the opportunities and hazards offered by the odds and thereby take advantage of them in actual play. But here, the adage, "A little learning is a dangerous thing," is something to be remembered. Familiarity with other dice games, most notably craps, may produce a distorted idea of how the odds operate in backgammon, where the features of the single roll and the double throws play significant parts.

All this becomes vital when playing for high stakes, which is a strong trend in modern backgammon. The strictly social backgammon player will find himself a sure loser if he guesses at the odds while serious players are analyzing them to exactitude. This may seem strange, considering that backgammon was popular among gamesters from Hoyle's day on, but safe plays were in vogue back then and the real dangers lay chiefly in being "gammoned" for double stakes, or "backgammoned" for triple stakes, which even a mediocre player could frequently avoid.

But modern backgammon has introduced a system of doubling the stakes, which a player can propose—or, in fact, demand—when he feels that it is to his advantage. His opponent can do the same, so this can raise the stakes to astronomical proportions, if carried to extremes, which sometimes can happen. So a checkup of the odds becomes all the more important and will be considered in brief before going into the doubling process.

Study the chart at the end of the previous chapter and you will see what all should know, that there are 36 possible combinations that can come up when the dice are thrown. Added, as shown in the "pyramid" that tops the chart, you can see how they range in totals from 2 to 12, reaching an apex at 7, which is something every crapshooter knows, or should know, though actually there are some who don't know it. Now that same chart applies to backgammon, but *only* when the desired total is so high —specifically 7 or above—that it requires a pair of dice to meet it.

Where the move depends upon a *single die,* it projects a different picture. Look at the chart and you will see that each individual number from 1 to 6 appears in eleven different combinations. To these you add the totals represented by a pair of dice; and also the 3s and 4s which a player gains when he rolls doubles. The total chances are shown in the lower chart and serve as a constant guide to good backgammon play.

There, you will note that a total of 1, which does not figure in many dice games, is very important in Backgammon, as the chances of throwing it are 11 out of 35, or almost 1 in 3. Going up the ladder, chances of gaining each successive number increase up to 6, which comes to 17 out of 36, making the odds almost even. But with 7, a number highly esteemed in other dice games, there is a sharp drop-off to 6 out of 36, or a mere chance of getting it in only 1 out of 6 tries. Number 8 offers the same odds as 7, but from there on, the chances dwindle, except for a slight lift with 12, which still only appears 3 out of 36 times, or 1 in 12 throws.

This shows that numbers 1 to 6 represent a danger zone, where blots are concerned. If Black should form a blot by moving a stone from his 8-point (8–B) to his bar-point (7–B), he would be giving White an almost even chance of hitting it, since a roll of 6 would enable White to move one of his back men from 1–B to 7–B. In contrast, if Black should move two of his stones from his 8-point to his bar-point, leaving the third as a blot on his 8-point (8–B), it would be practically a safety play, since White would have only one chance in six of hitting it with a 7 roll enabling him to move from 1–B to 8–B.

This explains why some players like to split their runners, or back men. It extends the danger zone to include more of the opponent's blots and it also increases the chances of a hit within the zone itself. If White should have his runners on 1–B and 2–B, he could hit a Black blot on 7–B with either a 6 or a 5, giving him 28 chances out of 36, which would be better than 3 out of 4. If a player wants his blots to be hit, as he often does when playing a back game, he can aid his aim by moving them into the danger zone instead of keeping them out of it.

Odds sometimes fool beginners when they carelessly form what they think are obvious conclusions. This applies particularly when reentering stones from the bar. Suppose that White has made 4 points on his inner table by placing blockers on 1–W, 3–W, 4–W and 6–W. Elsewhere, Black has a blot that he wants to advance as a builder, but he is afraid that White may hit it and send it to the bar. Getting back from there is what worries Black, because there are only 2 points on which he can reenter, 2–W and 5–W. That means that Black will have to roll a single 2 or 5, as combined totals won't do for a reentry.

Since White has four numbers, that leaves Black only two chances out of six, or one out of three, according to Black's casual calculation, so he decides not to risk his blot. If the odds were anywhere near even, Black would have chanced it; but not when they are two to one against him! Now, actually, the odds are better than even, in Black's *own favor,* as a reference to the chart will show. There are eleven ways of throwing 2 with a single die and eleven of throwing a 5, but two of those—2–5 and 5–2—are duplicated, so should be deducted. That leaves 20 out of 36 chances for Black to renter, which is definitely better than even.

You don't really need an actuarial mind to play backgammon, but it certainly can help your game. So a study of the odds is all-important and is almost second nature with most experts. It applies very strongly with the next item.

The Doubling Feature

This is what brought back backgammon and turned it into a modern game. It can also bring a player back into the game after he has sustained steady losses, or it can sink him deeper if he isn't careful. The procedure itself is very simple. Either player may offer to double the stakes when it becomes his turn to throw the dice. If his opponent refuses to double, the proposer wins the game and collects on a single basis.

If the opponent accepts the double, the game continues with doubled stakes, but it is now the opponent's turn to propose a new double or redouble, should he choose to do so. If he decides not to redouble, the game simply continues on its doubled basis, as the original proposer can not redouble until after his opponent has exerted the privilege. There are games, however, in which doubles and redoubles may be batted back and forth, reminding bystanders of a game of badminton rather than backgammon.

To keep track of how the doubling stands, serious players utilize a device called a "doubling block" which has the numbers 2, 4, 8, 16, 32 and 64 engraved on different sides. Whoever makes the first double brings the block to his end of the table and lays it with the 2 side upward. If his opponent later redoubles, it goes to the opponent's end and he turns the 4 side upward. This continues as long as redoubles are proposed and accepted. If declined, the final doubler wins and collects, then and there.

When to double depends a great deal on the player. Some experts will double when they see or sense a break in the game that others might not notice, just as a chess master recognizes a seemingly trivial advantage. If he waits until he has a fairly noticeable edge, a capable opponent is apt to accept the double even though he is behind, for this reason:

Suppose the opponent turned skittish and declined an early double four games in a row. The opponent would lose four games at single stakes, with no chance of redeeming them, except by going for doubles in other games, where he might run the risk of being redoubled. Now suppose that, instead, he accepts each early double, knowing that he still has a fair chance of winning the game. If he wins *just one* of those four games, he will will lose three doubles, or six, but he will win one double, or two. So he will lose the equivalent of four games, just as if he had declined the four, so he will be no worse off. But if good breaks enable him to win *two* of the doubled games, he will come out even, so it is worth it, if only as a sporting chance.

If a player waits too long before doubling, he will only defeat his own purpose. His opponent, being well behind, will be afraid of being gammoned, thereby losing the equivalent of two games anyway, which will jump to four if he is doubled. So he will naturally decline and the proposer will have to be satisfied with winning a single game, while if he hadn't tried to double, he might have gone on to win his gammon.

When both players are bearing off and are on the verge of a very close finish, doubling becomes extremely ticklish. Take a game where Black is about to roll with two stones left, on his 4-point (4–B) and his 3-point (3–B). White has just two left on his 5-point (5–W) and his 2-point (2–W). So far, neither has doubled, the game has been that close. Now, either can double.

In theory, Black shouldn't double, because his chances of bearing off both stones in one throw are a bit less than even. But Black knows that if his throw falls short, giving White another turn, White is apt to double because the odds are slightly in his favor. Therefore, a bold player in Black's position would double, figuring that if he doesn't, White will, but also hoping that he may scare White into refusing the double, for in that case Black would win a single game without risking a final throw.

Suppose White doesn't scare and accepts the double. So Black throws and flukes with a 3–2, which brings his two stones to his 1-point. So Black sits back and lets White throw, hoping that White will fluke, too, in which case Black will win, so it won't matter who doubled, Black or White.

But suppose that White, now in the saddle, decides to redouble. What then? Why then Black, being bold to start, might welcome it, since if White does fluke, Black will not only be a double winner, but will win four times over.

There are players, who, in Black's position, might decide to bait White into redoubling; but there are other players who, in Black's position, might feel that their luck had run out, so it would be better to let White take it without further struggle. Try it on your own backgammon board and see what you think.

Automatic Doubles

This is a form of doubling that depends on chance alone, being based on the business of each player throwing a single die to decide which is to make the first move according to the numbers on both dice. As stated earlier, if both dice show the same number, the players roll again, but with this proviso: Because the dice showed doubles, the game is played for double stakes. If the dice show doubles on the next roll, the stakes are redoubled; and if a third time, another redouble, though by then it might be wise to ask for another pair of dice. Or else a limit may be set on the number of automatic doubles allowable per game, three being the customary number. Automatic doubles are usually banned in games where players are allowed to double and redouble voluntarily, as already described.

Chouette

This is backgammon involving extra players. Each rolls the dice and the highest is designated as the "man in the box," taking on the rest as a team. The second highest roller becomes captain of the team and makes all the decisions after consulting with the other players. If the man in the box wins, he collects from each player and remains there for another game, while the captain goes to the foot of the team and the others move up a notch with a new captain taking over. If the man in the box loses, he pays off each player and goes to the foot of the team, while the captain becomes the man in the box and the players move up with a new captain taking over.

If the captain makes or accepts a double, other members of the team may act freely for the remainder of that game, dealing individually with the man in the box. If the captain refuses a double, other members of the team can accept it, with the highest ranking member acting as captain for the remainder of the game. If the team wins, the new captain becomes the man in the box. If the team loses, players move up according to their original rank, with the temporary captain taking his proper place.

VII

Acey-Deucy

THIS IS A MODERN FORM OF BACKGAMMON WHICH IS faster and more exciting than the original game. That is probably why it sprang to popularity in the United States Navy during World War II, and as a result has been remembered ever since. With the recent wave of interest in backgammon, acey-deucy has also experienced a revival, with a touch of nostalgia as well. Hence a detailed description of acey-deucy and suggestions for good play are given in the pages that follow.

The standard backgammon board is used, with fifteen stones, or "men," as they are more commonly called in acey-deucy. They follow the same routes, Black from 1–W to 12–W, then to 12–B and from there to 1–B; while White's direction is from 1–B to 12–B, then to 12–W and from there to 1–W. However, there is no setup to begin with. Instead, the board is entirely clear to start, with each player having his men stacked up in front of him. The players roll the dice as in backgammon; and with each roll, a player may enter one or more men, or move any after they are entered.

In the simple form of acey-deucy, there is no restriction whatever regarding entering and moving. If Black opens with a roll of 6–4, he can enter one man on point 6–W and another on 4–W; or he can enter a single man either on 4–W or 6–W, using the other die to move that man to 10–W. If he should roll a double 4, he counts the double twice, as in backgammon, giving him four moves of 4 points each. That means that he can enter one man on 4–W and move it to 8–W, then to 12–W; then to 9–B; or he can enter two men on 4–W and move both to 8–W; or move just one to 12–W; or he can enter three on 4–W and move one to 8–W; or he can enter all four on 4–W and leave them there.

This conforms with regular backgammon, but there is a special roll in acey-deucy which is exactly what the name of the game implies. If a player rolls 1–2, which consists of an ace (1) and a deuce (2), it is called "acey-deucy" and after entering or moving men to the tune of "one-two," he has the privilege of choosing and laying down *any double* that he wants and moving his men according to that count. In addition, he is given another roll of the dice to complete his turn.

As an example, Black, by rolling 1–2 to start could enter one man on 1–W and another on 2–W. He could then choose double 6, entering two more men on 6–W and moving them to 12–W. He would then roll the dice again and if they came up with 4–3, he might move the man from 2–W to 9–W; or he might move one from 1–W to 5–W and the other from 2–W to 5–W, establishing a block there. In contrast, he might decide to enter two more men on 3–W and 4–W. There are good reasons for any of these choices, which will be discussed in due course, but for the moment, a few more comments on the 1–2 roll are needed.

If Black should hit another 1–2 on his bonus roll (instead of the 4–3 already mentioned), it would count as another acey-deucy. He would move one man 1 point and another 2 points; or move just one for 3 points, whichever he preferred. Instead, he might enter a new man on 1–W and another on 2–W. After that he would again choose whatever double he wanted and use it for further moves or entries; and to top that, he would get another bonus roll. If that should happen to be another acey-deucy, the process would continue. In fact, it could go on and on, but don't bank on such things happening very often.

As the game continues and men begin to clutter up the board, a player sometimes finds himself unable to utilize his move.

In that case, the standard backgammon rule applies: The player must move as much as he can and simply forgo the rest. But with acey-deucy, this presents a special problem when a player makes a 1–2 roll. Say Black rolls 1–2 and enters his last two men on 1–W and 2–W. He tries to use a double 6, but finds he can't because of opposing blocks. In that case, he not only loses all or part of his 6–6; he is forced to forgo his bonus roll as well. However:

Often, he can get out of this bind by choosing a double smaller than 6–6. By using all four numbers of the lesser double, he may gain good positions and at the same time retain the right to his extra roll. A real problem develops, however, when a player is unable to use both numbers of a 1–2 roll. He must move one of the numbers if he can, but his acey-deucy terminates right there, as he loses his right to call a double and he is also denied an extra roll.

As in backgammon, the players can form "blocks" by putting two or more of their own men on a single point, with no limit as to the number that can be placed there. This prevents an opponent from ending a move on that particular point. A series of such blocks constitute a "blockade" which can prove difficult or impossible for an opponent to pass. A lone man placed on a point becomes a "blot" and can be "hit" or "knocked off" or "kicked off", just as in standard backgammon. In acey-deucy, such men are not ordinarily sent to the bar, because there would not be room for them there. A player simply adds them to his group of men that are still waiting to be entered.

Since these can be entered at any time, or held back while other men are being moved, the game of acey-deucy gives the players a tremendous leeway not found in backgammon. But as the game progresses through its various stages, it resolves itself into the final showdown, just as backgammon does. A player must bring all his men into his own inner table before he begins to bear them off. From then on, it is a question of one player taking them off faster than the other.

In backgammon, it has been noted that in "bearing off," the rolling of a double can suddenly give one player a special advantage, or turn what seems a losing game into a winner. The same applies to acey-deucy, but even more so, for this reason. If a player is bearing off and rolls an acey-deucy (1–2), he really hits the jackpot. The 1–2, though small, can often enable a player like Black to bear off two men from 1–B and 2–B. Then he gets the benefit of a big, big double, taking off four men in one swoop. To climax that, he has another roll which can help that much more, if he needs more help by then.

Superficially, acey-deucy starts as a running game, because a player has no alternative but to enter his men and advance them as runners, but he would get nowhere, if he persisted in that policy, as a wily opponent would knock off the blots as soon as they came within range. To protect his advancing men, a player must therefore establish blocks, as in backgammon, but he has none that are ready-made at the start. Therefore, to go into a blocking game, his purpose should be to get more than half his men on the board as soon as practical and establish points as far advanced as feasible, while keeping them close together.

In so doing, he should not outrun himself. For example,

Black, opening with a 6–5, might be overoptimistic if he entered on 6–W and moved to 11–W. If his next two rolls were 4–2 and 3–1, they would not suffice to bring a single builder up to support his blot on 11–W. If he started by entering one man on 6–W and another on 5–W, his next two rolls would enable him to establish a block on either 5–W or 6–W. Blocks are specially desirable at the outset, in case a player rolls an early double, as he can then move his blocks intact.

If Black should thrust a runner ahead to 11–W and White should push one to 8–B, Black might be inclined to use his next roll, 4–2 to move from 11–W to 8–B, hitting the White blot. That would be a real good start, but not for Black, as the chances are that White would be able to knock off the Black blot before Black could support it. As a result, Black would have used up two rolls of 11 and 6, a total of 17 points, to nullify White's single roll of 8 points. Such tactics seldom win a game of acey-deucy.

It takes a minimum of 25 points to enter a runner, bring it clear around the board and bear it off. Since a player has fifteen men, that multiplies to 375. Figuring the average throw of a pair of dice as 8 points, allowing for doubles, that would mean 47 throws at the very least, in order to complete a game. In backgammon, where most of the stones start from advanced positions, the theoretical minimum is only 167 or 21 throws, less than half the requirement in acey-deucy.

The message is clear. In acey-deucy, you must spend the time taken for a full backgammon game in order to attain the equivalent of a regular backgammon setup, but the board will be quite different. By bringing out more than half your men—better than eight out of fifteen—you should have soon established four blocks and by now should have five or even six. Your opponent may have about the same, resulting in a confrontation of forces concentrated about the middle of the board. The formations may vary. Often, opposing blocks are forced to move past one another; occasionally, each player is able to establish a prime, so that two blockades meet head on. That can't last long, and when it breaks, each player may find himself scrambling ahead of the other.

The objectives, of course, are to bring your men home and bear them off as in backgammon, but there is one factor to keep in mind as the game progresses. By holding back a few men instead of entering them, you automatically have a back game at your disposal, if or when you need it, so it is considered good strategy to hold one man in reserve as long as possible.

This brings up a question that is sure to arise with acey-deucy: "When a blot is hit, does the player have to reenter it in order to move his other men?" The answer is, "No, he does not," at least according to the way acey-deucy is generally played today. A rule demanding immediate reentry of a banished blot has been advocated in some circles, but it is probably a carry-over from a European form of backgammon from which acey-deucy was derived.

In regular acey-deucy, a man that has been "kicked off" can be reentered at any time, which means that it can be reserved for that purpose as long as desired.

The usual procedure in starting a game of acey-deucy is for each player to roll a single die. In case of a tie, each rolls again. Whoever rolls higher is the opener and throws both dice at his first turn. There is no automatic double to start, as sometimes used in backgammon, nor are there any gammons or backgammons in acey-deucy. However, in some games the stakes are automatically doubled when either player rolls an ace-deuce, though it is wise to put a limit on that. If desired, voluntary doubles may be allowed, using the standard doubling cube or its equivalent, as in backgammon.

One mode of scoring is for the winner to collect a specified stake, no matter how badly he defeats his opponent. This is specially applicable when any form of doubling is included. However, a more popular scoring system is for the winner to collect a chip or counter for each man that his opponent has left on the board, including any that he has not entered, making 15 the highest possible winning score. For those who would like something higher, the game can be played with the winner collecting a chip a point, according to the positions of the loser's men. A man on the loser's 1-point would cost him one chip; on his 2-point, two chips; and so on, back around the board, with a cost of 25 chips for any man that he has failed to enter.

Glossary

ACE-POINT Another term for a player's 1-point.

ACEY-DEUCY A roll of 1–2 with a pair of dice. Also, the name of a game in which such a roll gives a player a choice of doubles plus an extra roll.

AUTOMATIC DOUBLE An optional rule calling for doubled stakes if each player rolls an identical number (thus forming a double) at the start of a game.

BACK GAME One in which a player purposely sets up blots, hoping they will be hit and sent to the bar in order to supply him with more back men, stones, or counters.

BACKGAMMON A game in which the winner scores triple the value of a single game by bearing off all his stones before his adversary bears off any, and while the adversary still has a stone remaining on the winner's inner table or on the bar.

BACK MAN A stone on the opponent's inner table. The term is applied to each of the two stones originally placed on the opposing one-point, and also to any stones that are reentered after being hit and sent to the bar.

BACKWARD GAME Retaining back men to impede an opponent's rapid advance. Often the prelude to an intensive "Back Game."

BAR The divider between the inner and outer table, where blots are sent when they are hit.

BAR POINT A player's 7–point, just beyond the bar, therefore the first point in his outer table.

BATTLE OF BLOTS A game in which both players freely hit opposing "Blots."

BEARING OFF Moving stones from one's own inner table; allowable only after all have been brought there and retained there.

BLOCK Two or more stones placed on a single point, preventing the opponent from moving stones there.

BLOCKADE A series of blocks established by one player to impede his opponent's progress. Used specifically in Acey-deucy.

BLOCKING GAME One in which a player purposely forms blocks to halt an opponent's advance. Establishing a "Prime" by making six successive points is a great objective in this game.

BLOT A single stone on a point. Being unprotected, it can be hit by an opposing stone and sent to the bar, from which it must be reentered before its owner can make another move.

BOARD The entire layout used in the game of Backgammon; namely, a Backgammon Board. The term "Board" is also used instead of "table," as "inner board" for "inner table," or "outer board" for "outer table."

BONUS ROLL An extra roll of the dice taken by a player who rolls a 1–2 combination in the game of Acey-deucy.

BOX Position held by the lone player who takes on a team of adversaries in Chouette.

BUILDER A blot or additional stone placed in a position where it can be used to "make a point" or establish a block.

CAPTAIN Head man of a team of players who take on a single adversary in the game of Chouette.

CATCHERS Stones that have purposely been spread on various points in hope of catching an opposing runner on a coming roll and sending it to the bar. Valuable in a "Back Game."

CHOUETTE A form of standard Backgammon in which extra players form a team under the leadership of a Captain, opposing a lone player known as the "Man in the Box."

COME IN, OR COME ON To reenter a stone from the bar.

COMFORT STATION A nickname for the opponent's 12–point. So called, because a player has that point "made" to start, so his runners can stop off there, when he brings them from his opponent's inner table.

COVERING Making a point occupied by a blot by moving another stone to that same point, thus "covering" the exposed blot.

CUBE See Doubling Cube.

CUP Short for Dice Cup.

DICE Two cubes, with sides spotted from 1 to 6, which are rolled or thrown to determine the moves of stones on the Backgammon board.

DICE CUP A special cup from which dice are thrown in Backgammon.

DIE Singular for dice.

DOUBLE To increase the stakes of a Backgammon game to twice the original amount. Also used to signify "doubles" or "doublet."

DOUBLE GAME Another term for a "Gammon."

DOUBLES Rolls of the dice in which both come up with the same number, as 1–1, 2–2, 3–3, 4–4, 5–5, 6–6.

DOUBLET The original term for any one of the six possible doubles. A player rolling a doublet is allowed to count it twice. Thus 1–1 gives him four moves of one point each; 2–2, four moves of two points each; and so on.

DOUBLING CUBE A special cube, usually marked with the numbers 2, 4, 8, 16, 32, 64. Players alternate in doubling the stakes, turning up each successive number to indicate the increased total.

DOUBLING GAME The modern form of Backgammon in which players may voluntarily double the stakes during the course of play, according to specified rules.

ENTER To bring a man from the bar to the opponent's home board, according to the roll of a single die.

FLUKE A lucky roll of the dice upsetting normal calculations.

FORWARD GAME A game in which a player uses favorable rolls of the dice to advance stones as rapidly as possible without taking undue risks.

GAME To bring all a player's stones (men, checkers, counters) to his inner table and bear them off from there before the opponent can bear off all of his men.

GAMMON A game in which the winner scores double the value of a single game by bearing off all his stones before his adversary bears off any.

HIT To move a stone (man, checker, counter) to a point occupied by an opposing blot, sending the blot to the bar. Winning a single game of Backgammon is also termed a "Hit" (in contrast to a "gammon," or double game and a "backgammon" or triple Game.)

HOME BOARD A popular term for a player's inner table.

HOYLE COUNT An old-time way of determining which player is in the lead. A player counts any of his stones on his one-point as 1 each; any on his 2-point as 2 each; and so on, up to his 6-point. He then counts the number of points required to bring all his remaining stones to his 6-point. Next, he counts his adversary's stones in the same fashion and the smaller total tells which player is ahead, with the number of points by which he leads.

IDEAL ROLL The combination of 6–1 as an opening roll. A roll of 3–1 as an opener has a smiliar claim.

INNER TABLE The section of the Backgammon board that includes points 1 to 6. This, in turn, is subdivided into Black's inner table and White's inner table.

IN THE BOX Term used to designate the lone player who competes with a group in Chouette. He is known as the "Man in the Box."

KEY POINTS Points that most players like to "make" as soon as possible. In order of preference, these usually run: A player's own 5-point, or his adversary's 5-point; a player's own bar-point (7-point); a player's own 4-point.

KNOCK OFF To hit an opposing blot and send it to the bar. A term most commonly used in the game of Acey-deucy.

LOVER'S LEAP An opening or early move from the opponent's 1–point to the opponent's 12–point, as the result of a 6–5 roll of the dice.

MAKE A POINT To place two stones on the same point, thus preventing the opponent from ending a move on that point.

MEN Another term for the stones or counters (or checkers) used in Backgammon.

ODDS Various chances involving "hits," "making points," "Bearing off," and other features peculiar to the game of Backgammon and the rules governing the rolls of the dice.

OUTER TABLE The section of the Backgammon board that includes points 7 to 12. This, in turn, is subdivided into Black's outer table and White's outer table.

PLAYING SAFE Moving stones to points that a player has already made, rather than moving them to unoccupied points where they become unprotected blots.

POINT Any of the 24 elongated triangles on the Backgammon board on which stones are placed or moved during the course of play. The term also applies to a point which a player has made by placing two or more stones on it, which prevents his opponent from moving there.

POINT COUNT A method of evaluating a player's chances by adding the points on which his stones are stationed and subtracting their total from a similar count of the opponent's stones.

PRIME Six adjacent points made and held by one player, thus forming a barrier which his opponent can not pass.

RAIL Another term for the bar.

REDOUBLES In the Doubling Game, any doubles made following the first double.

REENTERING Bringing stones back from the bar; the same as entering, or coming in.

RUNNER A back man which a player is hoping to bring from his opponent's inner table by running it past any blocks set up by the opponent.

RUNNING GAME Outgrowth of a Forward Game, which becomes a full-fledged running game when a player gets all his stones past opposing blocks, so he can run them all to his inner table and bear them off from there.

SAFETY PLAY To make a lesser point, or move stones to points already held, rather than risk leaving "Blots" by advancing stones too rapidly.

SEVEN-POINT The first point in a player's outer table. Also termed the "bar point."

SPLITTING RUNNERS To move one runner ahead of its companion.

STONE A counter or man used in Backgammon.

TABLE A portion of the Backgammon board.

TAKING OFF The same as bearing off.

THROW A roll of the dice, particularly when a cup is used.

THROW OFF Another term for bear off.

TRIC TRAC or TRICK TRACK An old name for Backgammon.

TRIPLE GAME Another name for a Backgammon.

WALKING A PRIME To move a prime (of six adjacent blocks) along the board by adding extra stones from in back to supplant others that are moved to the front. The same applies to a partial prime and especially to a blockade in Acey-deucy.